# A Walk in My Moccasins

## Memoirs of a Deaf Physician

By Justus Peters MD

A Walk in My Moccasins

Memoirs of a Deaf Physician

By Justus Peters MD

ISBN-13: 978-1470007058
ISBN-10: 1470007053

Cover Art: Static rhythm #2
Artist: Sandra Peters

Design, Layout, and Typesetting
by Alexander Becker
www.alexanderbecker.net

*Dedicated to my family.*
*Thanks, you are my world.*

# Contents

# Prologue

Words seem unable to describe both fortunate and unfortunate events that enabled me to find my goal in life. Living in a quiet peaceful world void of confrontation did not assuage my inner turmoil. Every day I struggled to understand the simplest of tasks. My demons held my joy captive while I suffered daily anxiety about what people are saying. I kept wondering "why are people whispering all the time?"

They looked at me and said something, and slowly their faces would change as I failed to hear what they said. First, a questioned expression that slowly changed to worry, and inevitably to pity. I was ashamed. I fiercely attempted to understand what people were saying. The changing expressions, lips, eyes, faces were all recorded into my memory. I learned how tongues would touch the top two teeth when the sound „th" was made, I observed intensely over time to learn more words.

I differentiated how the lips would purse together differently with the "b" and "p" sounds. Naïve to the pity others felt, I continued to struggle. I became angry with God. Mom would take me to pastor after pastor to try to heal me. I still couldn't hear. My mom's desperate attempts to get me healed made me both hopeful when I was younger, but also resentful at the many failed attempts.

Imagine waking up to an alarm clock but it is just a low hum. Imagine walking to the bathroom and not hearing anything. In the dark, you are all alone with no sound. When the water runs in the shower or the sink, you can't hear the splash. Even when you talk everything is muted. When people talk, you can see their mouths moving, and just a little low decibel sound, but no important sounds to determine what word was actually said. Even when adults would get eye level with you, you couldn't hear everything.

When I did hear something very well, it was a shock. Every once in awhile, dad would yell, and I could hear everything he said. The experience was new and terrifying for a deaf child to hear.

But no matter what happened, mom always reassured me that everything was going to be okay. That motherly confidence vote kept me going despite the trials and tribulations of my childhood.

A Walk in My Moccasins is a book I pray that gives others hope to continue on with their dreams. I want to contribute back to society that has given me the chance to succeed. I've been blessed in many ways knowing that in this country, having a disability does not limit your chance for success. And I pray that many of you readers will find heartwarming stories through the ups, downs, trials and tribulations I have endured to be where I am today.

# Chapter 1

## An Amazon Woman and the Boy Half Grown

*Silence*

*No trickling of water on the rocks,*
*Nor song of birds in springtime love,*
*Nor chimes of old timer clocks,*
*Nor chorus of rains from skies above,*
*No hum of motors going by,*
*No laughter, nor crying anywhere,*
*Nor conversing,*
*Floating through the thick black,*
*No sound no sound no earthly sound.*
*The invisible cocoon around,*
*I walk and feel just inside thoughts,*
*Which seem beneath the ground,*
*Leaning on the beamless trees,*
*A darkened gleam of endless seas,*
*No one seems to see me here,*
*No sound no sound no earthly sound.*
*The wind wills itself against my ears,*
*A distant hum throughout the years,*
*Changing lips and faces too,*
*Nothing changes nothing's new,*
*It's all the same again and now,*
*No sound no sound no earthly sound.*

*Justus Peters MD*

From my youngest memories two things my mother always said about my birth. One was that the obstetrician called her an, "Amazon Woman." I was also "half grown." I was the largest of 4 children that mom enjoyed delivering. She always reminds us of how she "enjoyed" the entire labor process.

This woman loved being pregnant! She loved having kids. When my wife, Donnette, told her that she is getting an epidural, mom scowled. She also doesn't mind telling everyone how long she enjoyed nursing her children. Much to the siblings and my chagrin, she still shares this very personal information with strangers.

I was a pleasant baby. Mom said I would sit for hours playing with my own toys on the ground and rarely said a peep. But as I grew older and words were taught to me, mom and dad became worried. In my baby book mom writes a gradual onset of understanding of my deafness:

*"Justus isn't affected by what anyone expects of him. He is very creative, a little impulsive, more sanguine temper, enjoys fun so much!" Mom wrote in my Baby Book.*

*"He says, "Yion," for "Lion," "Hore," for "Horse," and "Dang-ooh," for "Thank you!" She wrote again on the next page. She never thought the cute pronounciations were results of high decibel hearing loss.*

*August 8, 1976: "Justus is really developing into a sweet child. He listens to me when I give him a command. He only needs for me to correct him with words mostly.*

*He respects the word, "No." His eyes are big and brown-the color of Don's. His hair is blonde to red on the ends. He seems slimmer than Marion but longer and still stout anyway. Justus is pleasant and rare, always full of fun and a sweet smile. He plays extremely well, and gets tickled at little things."*

This last sentence really hits the spot. I still get ticked at the little things. One thing about being deaf is that whenever you hear a joke or something funny, you almost die laughing. I missed so many jokes without my hearing aides, that when my patients say something funny, I really bust a lung. My joking years were lost during my growing up stages sort of like a comedy show that I completely missed out on.

*June 7, 1977: "Justus is a very precious and dear son. His personality is contagious-fusses back when disciplined, very compassionate, and quick to forgive."*

*June 12, 1977: "Justus is going through 'terrible two's.' He is so demanding. He knows what he wants. He says, 'T.D,' for 'T.V,' and 'pok,' for 'pop.' He smiles so sweetly, and plays for long periods of time, and loves books."*

At 4 years old, complete sentences should be enunciated well. Imagining all the possible words a 4 year old person can say, I wondered what I was doing verbalizing so poorly. What was the first clue? For mom I wondered if she questioned herself the many times she sat down to write in the baby book. For dad who rarely was home when I was cognizant, I wondered what his first clue was. When asked most recently, he told me.

He said, *"I would whisper in your ear just moving my lips. When I noticed you moving your lips without making sound, I knew you had a hearing problem."*

Visualizing a toddler ambling around just moving his lips seemed benign, but as sharp as my dad was, he could tell.

My mother had already raised a gentle boy to the age of 4, when I was starting to speak more clearly. She saw the television shows, the pediatrician advice columns, and the many textbooks on "How to's" on raising kids. She became curious whenever she spoke my name behind my back, and I wouldn't respond. Furthermore, she couldn't get my attention unless she looked into my eyes. Not surprisingly, even clapping her hands behind my back close up wouldn't startle me.

*March 1978: "Justus is adorable-calls 'waffles,' 'awfuls.' He runs on tippy toes when happy."*

*April 3 1979: "Still can't pronounce 'truck,' says, 'fruck.' He is very stubborn but dearly sweet. He is a little pack rat. Has his stuff in hall closet."*

Among the many mispronounced words and phrases, were the actions that I exhibited in public and in solitude. Mom witnessed me happily playing in my own little world while alone, and ignorant of other peoples' "praise," of how cute and chubby I was. I didn't show off when other people expressed interest, and I didn't get that nervous around new folk. My brother picked on me either by scaring me, or using me as a punching bag with his panda puppet. Much to his chagrin I couldn't be scared unless he jumped in front of me. I often wondered if watching a deaf person in a horror movie would be either boring or surprising. By the time I was grown, I would have made quite a boring horror movie star candidate. Not because of my screaming ability, but rather by the fact that I was so paranoid and cautious to decrease any potential scare.

Her last entrance was after they discovered I had hearing loss:

*May 1981: "Justus has inoperable inner ear damage-40 decibels is what he hears. We must get hearing aides. But he is a trooper."*

It was her last entrance. The rest of the baby book was blank or had various scribbles of my own with crayolas and poor pensmanship on childhood pictures. It seemed as if it became the beginning of the end for mom to acknowledge my childhood. Maybe it was denial that I now was abnormal. The official report created an emotional battle for my mom, and by stating I am "a trooper," she hoped optimistically I would be brave in the impending warfare with society. Maybe it was her own false reassurance.

The audiologist at the Pawnee Indian Clinic was a middle aged man with glasses, and a warm smile. The referral from the pediatrician was in question to my behavior. The many missed terms, the ignorances, the clues, and perhaps the most important of all, the very limited vocabulary succumbed to inevitability. The test results were not surprising -- bilateral moderate to severe hearing loss of sensori-neural origin was the diagnosis. Whatever went through mom's mind with the diagnosis, I do not know. I wondered if she thought maybe I would be on lifelong welfare, an illegitimate citizen, or if I was going to be home-bound the rest of my life. What things did she learn?

Looking back at the statistics of Sensori-neural hearing loss, it was not optimistic. Did mom feel reassured with the knowledge at the time? It isn't common, only 1-3 per 1000 newborn infants are born with hearing impairment. The average age of detection was around 14 months, yet I was 5 years old in May 1981. I am still not sure if the earlier detection could have made an impact on my communication skills, or my educational attainment. It might have helped with my quality of life by improving my self-esteem.

# Chapter 2

## The Boy with Ears of an Elephant

*Once Again Move*

*If becoming brave makes a man,*
*Or strength and willing to make a stand,*
*And trails of tears I have to go,*
*Or uphill battles fought from below,*
*This rite of passage I hope will prove,*
*The hearts of weak will once again move.*

*Justus Peters MD*

Did my hearing impairment prepare me for what lies ahead? Out of all the medical conditions I have learned about, I feel most specialized in hearing loss. I wonder still if medical students are prepared effectively on the special considerations needed in caring for children with hearing loss.

Mom learned as much as she could about my problem. She told me she read microfilm, watched special health alerts and updates on the field of medicine and audiology. She knew I was going to need special care and speech therapy. Like any parent she wanted to do the best possible for her children. She never told me she felt guilty, nor placed blame on anything or anyone. What could be said for her, could not be said for my dad. She often skirted around this issue. She wouldn't tell me exactly what dad felt about my hearing. I don't know if she was protecting me like always, or whether she just didn't want to say anything bad about him. *"Dad had some difficulties,"* she stated simply.

Whatever difficulties evolved into my family, I initially thought was my fault. I guessed mother's strength held my dad's sanity in place. She was the one at home making sure I was ok. She was the one with me building me up everyday. Whether or not, he felt it his fault, he did feel guilty. Once a parent discovers a problem with their child, naturally they try to blame themselves. I remember mom saying it may have been the German Measles, but that would have caused a condition known as Congenital Deafness Syndrome, a much more serious problem than mine.

Dad seemed to bury his anxieties and fear into his work. He always worked overtime to provide for our little family, and I wonder if he felt himself a failure for having not one, but two children with a disability. The family went through difficulties too. Three years after my diagnosis, my dad separated from the family. He left us in Arkansas. I remember mom sobbing in the master bedroom, and all 4 of us children on the big bed crying. To listen to a mother loudly sob, scream, and flail at a telephone, was torturous to witness. The scene still can replay in my memory today.

If my hearing deficiency was bad, my sense of smell was worse. To compensate, I needed to literally place my nose inches away from the food. This helped discern the aromas of the food. One time, my grandmother smacked me on the back of the head so that my face went into a dish of mashed potatoes. She traumatized me with stuff like that all the time. I always heard her well because she yelled at me at the top of her lungs like she was scaring away a monster.

"GET YOUR FACE OUT OF THE FOOD!!" she roared, in her gravelly voice from too many years of smoking and alcohol.

Because the world to me was a low continuous hum that was soft, I became very sensitive to loud noise. If a live band were playing I would cover my ears. In traffic, I never winced until I received hearing aids at 19 years of age. Even nowadays when I am in traffic walking between buildings, I turn off the aids so as to protect what little hearing I have left.

One thing my mother did to me was always take me by both arms and smile into my face before speaking. It comforted me and gave me a very good reason to read her lips. With mom, I never felt guilty when I couldn't hear her. She understood my issues, and she empathized naturally. When she learned about my hearing deficit, she wasn't too worried, because I was a boy. But when my youngest sister was born with the same problem, she was worried because *"the world is harder on girls."* I look at Becky now, and she is just as hardy as I am. We've been through the ringer, and didn't know what is normal. We learned on our own what the cultural norm is, and feeling outcast enabled us to reach deep inside and find strength and not to rely on others so much.

My sister and I share a bond unlike most siblings, because we both have the same disability. No one can understand us like we can. It shows in the pictures how her and I are very close. Becky was almost like my twin. We became movie going partners, we lived together for awhile, and it broke our hearts to depart.

Reading lips isn't a hard thing to do. I simply associate a vowel or consonant sound with the shape of the lips at the time it is vocalized, and a word pops into my head. Sometimes people will be talking to me and I will be in the same room with them, and I won't hear them, so they would start laughing at me.

Mom was the best communicator out there for me. She supported me in all my events and projects. She helped me with Boy Scouts by taking me to troop meetings, and learning new things. She took me to Vacation Bible School and although it was embarrassing, she spoke to each of my teachers about my need and handicap. She somehow always worked me into a desk up front closest to the teacher. This way, I wouldn't have to see what others were doing behind my back. It was very easy to ignore any snickering, since I couldn't hear it anyway.

When the time came to get my first hearing aids, I remember going to the same place.

The Pawnee Indian clinic was a small brown stone building which always smelled like antiseptic spray inside. After multiple appointments, spending many mornings and afternoons in a sound booth listening for sounds and repeating words back to the best of my ability, it was time. It wasn't a surprise that I had some sort of deficit. So when I turned 6, I finally became fitted. I have a lot to owe Pawnee Indian Clinic. Small town Pawnee, Oklahoma was my hero in 1981. Six years is a long time to be without the ability to hear high decibels.

The pink bubble gum smelling jelly that was squeezed into my ear to make a hearing aide mold completely blocked out any noise. The audiologist would gently remove it after a minute, and sound would return in a low hum. I could hear but hearing was limited to low frequency sounds. Men were easier to hear than women, who had higher frequency sounds. Some of the consonants and vowels have different frequency sounds as well. I could hear a faint "b" but it sounded close to a "t" or "c", but with lip reading I learned how people make noises and am able to decipher which actual consonant came out.

Higher frequency sounds like "t" or "c" usually were missed even if I read lips. Men spoke in lower frequencies and in higher decibels so not only could I hear them better, I could carry on conversations with them. I had about 50% loss in both ears, and as time went on, I lost more.

My experience with more normal hearing was very limited. I could point out much more detail from when I resumed hearing aid use at the age of 19.  What I do remember very well at 6 years-old, includes the bullying by classmates.

Kids pointed at me and laughed. I remember a boy in 2nd grade who tormented me. He wore a black leather jacket and had very light blond hair. The kids all laughed at me and I shared the humiliation with a classmate with cerebral palsy who had a very abnormal walk. It shamed me to the point of anger.

I started speech therapy in first grade, and loved my teacher in Cabot Arkansas at Westside Elementary. Everyday, I was called "Elephant Ears," by my classmates, and this affected me. Growing up resentful and hard, I wondered why bullies do what they do. Did it make them feel better? Empower them? This affected me to the point I decided to be creative with art.

Drawing and coloring classmates in disfigured bodies released my anger. I drew comics of heroes in ninja world, or western world. The heroes all had hearing problems like my own. It was as if making a hero disabled, made it real and possible for me to be a hero in the future. Needless to say, I never became an artist.

My Elephant Ears' nickname never wore off and got old very quick for me. I started resenting not just my classmates, but also my hearing aids, and my mother for putting me through such torture. I would cry sometimes and lie out in the field on top of a big circular hay bale and pretend that God would take me up in a fiery chariot like Elijah. And although that never happened, I planned and fought with my inner demons.

After many days of self pity, my plan emerged. I would put my hearing aids in my jeans and forget about them, allowing them to make their final journey to the washing machine. I secretly hid my hearing aides in my jeans and put them in the laundry, where mom subsequently washed and then dried the clothes.

After a few days, my mom walked up to me with something in her hand. Observing the shattered hearing aids in her palm did nothing to me. After resenting the hearing aids so much, I felt relief at their destruction. I felt maybe I would be normal if I didn't have to wear the "elephant ears." Not wanting to explain why the hearing aids were shattered, I feigned ignorance. But mom saw right through me. The disappointed face is one I will never forget. I always strove to make her and dad happy.

The disappointment acted like a mirror of guilt in which I could see the nastiness of what I had become. I couldn't trick mom, she always knew better. She told me she found them in the dryer. I felt bad for lying to mom. She has known for awhile now, and she reminds me of my trickery whenever I get out of line. Mothers always have ways of humbling their children. Whether it be reminding of length of breastfeeding, labor, or both, and that is in front of company. More people know me intimately than I would care to know, because of mom's knack for sharing information.

Even with my office staff, she couldn't keep to herself this very personal information. My sibs and I have heard the story many times. It goes something like:

"This is Rebecca, you know how long I nursed her?" Mom would entertain a friend with a sly smile.

*"Oh, I could only imagine."* They would always say.

*"4 years!"* She cried out with laughter.

My sibs and I always wanted to run from the room to escape such agony. As we got older, we just rolled our eyes and said, "Oh Mother." I think the most recent time she shared the personal information was with my office staff this year.

My brother enjoyed having the upper hand in many of the games we played. He would hide in the woods and I would be wondering aimlessly trying to find him, undoubtedly making a lot of racket. Marion would jump out and scare me from behind every time. He did that in the house as well. My brother became adept at sneaking around that he developed a "sniper" mentality. He delightfully practiced his soldier ways on me.

My mom and dad would test my hearing by clapping their hands behind my back when I was not paying attention. I try to imagine what they thought when I didn't respond. Did they feel ashamed at their disabled son? Did they have sadness for any future plight I would have to endure? Mom told me that Dad was very upset with my hearing loss. I can understand. A father wants a fit son who is genetically perfect. Life doesn't always work that way I learned.

Living quietly allowed me to have a very vivid imagination. My mom remembers when I would hang out in my room for hours upon hours playing with little toys and robots. I developed empires for little paper robots. I developed multiple story lines with my Star Wars and GI Joe action figures. I read novels, and westerns, so my little paper transformers were developed into different universes.

I had little guys for my westerns, mafia, and for music bands, football, and medieval universes. I wasn't too violent as a child. I would use little spit balls and blow them at the little guys to exercise that imaginative violence.

Hours upon hours I spent alone playing with my toys and my imagination. It made no sense to watch television. I couldn't hear it anyway. Talk about an exercise in futility, trying to lip read a conversation was driving me nuts. When I did watch it, sitting up close to the television was the only way for me to get any information. I have family photos that show me sitting in a small chair up close to the television.

# Chapter 3

## Big Wheels and Black Cats

*A Quiet*

*Quite a quiet night,*
*No sound in sight,*
*Just windless flight,*
*Toward the twilight.*

*Justus Peters MD*

One of my favorite memories was when I was a boy scout. I loved being everything about being a scout. I loved the badges, the honor, and fun activities. Building projects helped me to see results. These results increased my confidence. What little confidence I had was buried in my creative play. My creative play included the comics, the toys, the paper made transformers, and all allowed me to escape the doldrums of reality. During elementary school I always played by myself at recess.

The Boy Scouts helped me find a calling, or a home and enabled me to be socialized with other kids. When the socialization began, I learned I had lacked many things that could have fulfilled me for so long, including camaraderie, social skills, and feeling needed. When that feeling arose, it brought forth desire.

That desire to achieve was the seed that was nurtured with my ambition. My ambition to prove what I am capable of achieving despite my disabilities seemed to frame my destiny. I believe it was the Boy Scouts that helped me get there.

The Boy Scout Troop in Cabot Arkansas was an active organization. I remember saluting the flag and reciting the Pledge of Allegiance in the standard Scout salute. I remember in uniform at meetings in the front of the large cafeteria at school.

My brother, Marion ("Roo"), was much better at it than I was. You could put him in a forest by himself and he could live off the land. On the other hand, I might not make it. I hope to think in the back of my mind, Marion learned to be self sufficient by testing me and see how I failed before he endeavored himself to a task. But I feel that is wishful thinking.

The Troop was the first time I began to feel proud of some real accomplishments. To think that I was so bored from deafness, I was reaching out for anything to build self esteem.

In Arkansas at night dad would help us catch lightning bugs and put them in jars. We would keep those jars in the garage and watch their little lights flicker. Dad always had a fire-work display during the 4th of July. He would aim bottle rockets and roman candles over the fence and field. When he lit the black cats, my broth-er and I would act like we were storming Oma-ha Beach. He always had this burning cigarette hanging out of his mouth while the family sat watching his work. He stood there next to all the fireworks and put on the display for us.

While in Cabot, one of my favorite memo-ries was of dad driving us kids in his white Toy-ota truck and doing donuts in the snow out in the front yard and we would just hang onto each other for dear life. He would bring home some Big Wheel tricycle toys and Roo and I would race each other on our very large drive way. Roo was such a gifted athlete, he could beat me at anything and everything. I think the only times I ever won, was because he let me.

We staged regular WWF wrestling bouts and use the master bedroom king size bed to pummel Becky with various duplexes or body slams. Marion and I had boxing matches where we used animal puppets for our gloves and the soft heads of the puppets were the only thing keeping me conscious from all the head pummeling I got from him.

My younger sister Elizabeth, was such a girly girl, she was always in her room playing with her Barbies, and sucking on her "bankie," and sniffing the sides until she found the right area and started furiously sucking again.

Being hard of hearing was difficult for my early love life. It is true that I had daydreams of girls as early as 3rd grade. When I was in 3rd grade I fell in puppy love with the cutest girl in the class. To my despair, the popular boy in class staked his claim during a party telling us that he loved her.

Socially inept, I crept through school. I couldn't hang out in a group because I couldn't tell who would be talking at any one time. I was better at one on one conversation. I went to a speech therapy class. That taught me that being different was ok. The other students in the special education class seemed to have learning difficulties with me.

It was in special education that I learned how to use the computer. Hearing little forced me to utilize my hands and my eyesight more. I became quite adept at mathematics, spelling, and other learning games.

Anything visual stimulated my mind. I was able to see a math problem and within a second I was typing in the answer on the keyboard. Tournaments were put on in our entire 4th grade class. That most popular boy ended up playing me in the final for the class computer whiz crown. I won and therefore obtained my retribution for the "baby heartbreak" he caused me. I won this invisible ink marker which enabled me to write whatever I wanted unseen to others. I would then utilize a different marker to reveal what I had written. In 4th grade, this was a most awesome prize.

I continued lip reading in my quiet world. The quietness was pervasive. Imagine a very boring room with the only sound coming from an air conditioning unit. When noise doesn't exist, you find it difficult to concentrate sometimes. Your eyes search other faces, other items to catch your interest. You silently hope for conversation, something important. You search for worldliness when there seems just space. You search for meaning when there seems such placidity. You search for energy when it seems all is calm.

The siblings and I would play "school," and give each other homework to do and then grade the papers. I loved math so much, most of my homework for my siblings was math problems.

I went through a major health issue regarding a bone tumor on my right cervical rib. I had a major operation that left my right arm useless, so I had to learn to write left handed. I even had to play dodgeball by throwing with my left hand. Still to this day, my right arm is not as strong as my left. The brachial plexus nerve highways were disrupted somehow in order to get to the cervical rib. The tumor was benign, but made a large deformity on my neck, therefore the entire rib was removed.

Often the experiences of medical care seemed to be the catalyst that prompted me to go for being a physician, but it still remained an unfathomable dream, an impossible journey, and a never-ending trial. Sometimes small bumps on the road of life led me down a different path, eventually leading to the field of medicine.

The Space Shuttle was hugely popular in the 80s while I grew up. Dad brought us to Little Rock, Arkansas to see Challenger fly overhead on top of a Boeing 747. When the Space Shuttle went up it was so hugely popular, my dad bought a model of it. He spent hours and hours on that thing. Wondering what happened to the model, I hoped I never tossed it into the air. Whatever dad tried to do, he always tried to perfect it. He started many projects, but finished few. Those he did finish were perfect.

As a child, I only saw dad cry a couple times. Once was when we thought Elizabeth was missing, and the other time was when the Shuttle exploded January 28, 1986. Although I wasn't there with dad when the shuttle exploded since my parents were separated at the time, he still cried about it when he visited not long after. Mom and the kids lived in Fame, Oklahoma, and dad lived up in Wichita, Kansas. We went to a small country school at Stidham, which had 2 grades in each classroom. In 4th grade, I was in the same class as my cousin Shane Kemp in the 3rd grade.

Those days we took the bus, and one of my favorite memories as a child was coming home to mom every day after the long bus ride from school. She would have fresh cookies and milk waiting for us.

Mom said my creativity was very deep. I could fold up a cardboard box, cut a couple holes in it, and play all day with my Star Wars and GI Joe figures acting like it was a huge space ship.

Dad helped with making our little race cars for the troop meetings, and it was like watching magic happen before our eyes. We saw dad carefully cut the wood out, weigh the wood, melt some lead to make the cars "legal" so that we were all the same size. He then helped Marion and I paint and lacquer up the cars. My car was blue, and Marion's was red. Dad always helped us with these little projects. What a guy he was. He still is my hero.

As much as I loved dad, and tried in vain to impress him, I always found a way to get put back in the doghouse. As an adventurous kid, I wrecked dad's sweet white Chevy truck when I was just five years old. It seems hard to believe that I could do it without truly driving the vehicle. The memory of the steep driveway in Sherwood Arkansas remains clear to this day. I didn't realize it then, but I released the emergency brake, and the truck slammed into the garage door.

Earning badges and honors improved not only my self-esteem, but also my ambition. Mom helped me with some of the little activities. But ambition clouded my judgement several times during Boy Scouts. I fibbed on some of the activities just to get more badges. At an early age, I wish I had learned more about integrity. Nowadays, it is my favorite word. I failed at that at an early age not because I didn't learn what not to do, but rather because I didn't learn consequences of what I had done. I didn't know if I had that lesson when I was a child or not. Looking back, I feel remorseful, but it isn't like I knew what I was doing at that age.

Like I said — I wanted those badges. I didn't know how to make a campfire, but I could read the instructions. Mom asked me if I made a campfire, *"yes,"* I answered. She would then simply sign the page without following up on it. This was one of many failures I regret doing. As a father, I would be so ashamed of my son. But it allowed me to see what I was capable of doing and what I needed help on. Now I know that if I was going to sign the line, then my son or daughter will prove that they can build a campfire.

Obviously, I needed more help than the average person, as I couldn't hear the lessons, and we didn't have many resources to fulfill most of the activities in the Scout manual.

I became resourceful however, and played with fire many times. I became the family "garbage man." I would carry all the garbage out to the dump. We had several large 55 gallon barrels in various stages of rusted break down. Subsequently, I'd light the garbage on fire, and watch it burn. Observing flames was a chore, and it was worse when garbage flew out onto the ground and started a fire accidentally. I fought many fires with the local volunteer fire fighters. For a young boy, these large fires were pretty traumatic. One time, a hair spray can was left in the garbage and it exploded while I was near the barrel. My hair had singed curlies all the way around.

The fact that the house didn't burn down amazes me to this day. Thanks to dad's smoking habit, we found lighters all over the place. We didn't need flint rock or wood to start a fire. We could light rolls of paper and run through the house with the smoke trails behind us acting like we were a mob. Marion, who I affectionally called Roo, and I would wear towels around our necks like capes, and run from room to room acting like Superman and Batman.

To this day, Roo doesn't recall ever running through the house with a roll of paper on fire. Perhaps that was my subconscious trying to validate the crime with another person? Our Cabot home was long red brick. We could run from one side of the house to the other in about 10 seconds. I am still so amazed we didn't burn that house down.

We moved to Kansas, and I raised Buff Orpinton chickens when we lived out in the country. My first batch of 50 chicks would chirp all day in their little cardboard box. I never tried, but found a way to lose a chick here and there. Friends would come over with little toddlers and a couple would be squeezed to death by a toddler. A cat would get a hold of another.

My dad built a couple of chicken pens for me. One of our family dogs was a large Saint Bernard named Roscoe. He looked exactly like "Cujo" in the movie based on a Stephen King Novel. This dog found a way to tear open a chicken pen, and killed the entire first batch of chickens. We drove home, and it was like coming to a scene in a war with little yellow bodies laying all over the yard and driveway. I took awhile to completely get over that numbness.

Being just a naïve boy, I was still too young to think, *"why me."* I just wondered why a dog would kill so many precious things. It was a window into reality. Animals do evil things. When Roscoe attacked our Tennessee Walker Horse, Saucy, chewing her face and ear, we employed a neighbor farmer to come over to our house and put Roscoe down. I'll never forget the sound of the gunshot and that exact moment. I didn't understand why, when God had the power to give and take life, that men did the same.

My second batch died in a fire. I remember mom walking in to my room around 6 o'clock in morning and she smelled like smoke. I remember the moment like it was yesterday. I can still close my eyes and smell that smoke on ma. Tears were making clear lines down her ash blackened face. When she told me, I didn't say anything. I almost knew it was going to happen. I felt sick because it almost made me feel like I was not taking care of my babies.

I learned the hard way to take responsibility seriously. For some reason, my parents believed in me enough to try a third time. This time, dad built a pen off the ground to keep out ferrets, snakes and weasels. Although I lost some of my third batch, I kept some too. I was finally successful at something other than a great imagination.

When those chickens grew big enough, I showed them at 4-H fairs. I would shine their claws, and wax their combs. Getting those blue ribbons always made me proud. One night, my dad got tickled at how I said, *"Poultry."* I said, *"poetry."* He corrected me, no, *"pole-tree."* He pointed at a telephone pole, and then he would point at a tree while verbalizing the words loud enough for me to hear. I then knew how best to say the word.

My dad and mom delighted in listening to me pronounce words even into my older years. They pointed to a local bar sign that read, "Rendezvous." They asked me how to pronounce it. Never having seen the word before, I said, *"rendeezahvus."* They howled in laughter.

For one of our 4-H group nights, we did a lip sync concert of 50s music for the audience. I had a bass guitar, lead was played by Eddie, and Louie on the drums. We played in the Watermelon Festival talent show in front of the whole city. I am embarrassed when I see the old picture of me with a "see through" shirt that was too large, fake playing a bass guitar. But it was fun.

My first kiss was Heather Ward in Oxford, Kansas. We did it under the bridge on top of the Arkansas River. I was pressured as it was those days when Truth or Dare was a serious game. You had to be brave to play Truth or Dare. If a dare wasn't performed, you were laughed at. And at that time the ultimate bravery was kissing another girl. But if you could complete a dare, you were respected.

She was also my first sweetheart while in 5th grade. She had brown hair that was straight when I first met her, but became curly with time. Her big hazel eyes sometimes bellied something sinister when she half smiled. It was a game we boys played on each other all the time. I had no interest in girls in middle school, or at least the interest in kissing them. We wrote each other many times even after I moved away to Oklahoma.

Maybe it was the fact dad was a workaholic, but I don't know why I worked so hard. When one can't hear, we learn to become self sufficient. I learned early that the harder I worked, the more rewards I got. The harder I performed, the more doors would open up. I never felt entitled to anything. Dad provided a roof and food. Mom was a loving parent. We received new clothes once a year for the new school year. Mom painted her Native American Trail of Tears paintings, and Dad worked forever.

Dad always was reading. He would come home, sit in his big living room chair and open up his book. My dad was my hero, so naturally I had the desire to be like him. I studied him, and sometimes found him in the bathroom on the toilet reading a book. He was always reading! If we asked him a question while he was reading a book, he would keep reading until the end of the paragraph, put his finger on the point where he left off, take a deep breath, and exhale exasperatedly, and finally look up at us. Naturally, he had great answers for the most mundane questions we had. He was a walking dictionary, thesaurus, and book worm.

He read Dick Francis, Dean Koontz, Lawrence Sanders and other fiction authors. For Christmas he would buy the newest Dick Francis novel and then give it to my aunt. He was conservative, but never political. He was a Baptist minister and went to Seminary in Fort Worth before being promoted in the corporate world through Skaggs Alpha Beta. We moved all over the Midwest.

In school I was average. I made bad grades in some classes. In fact, my first "F" came in 4th grade. I didn't feel bad about it, but with time, I learned that there was a direct proportion of how a teacher looked at me when I did well on an assignment compared to how a teacher treated me when I did poorly. Being a visual learner, I liked it more when I was treated nicely, and being extremely sensitive at the time, I worked very hard to please the teachers. They were making miracles everyday by being understanding and patient with me. Knowing I was hearing impaired, they worked closely with me.

We moved from good schools to bad schools and back to good schools, so I received a very broad scope of education. The small rural schools in Oklahoma were slightly behind the urban schools of Arkansas, but slightly better than the rural schools in Kansas and so on and so forth.

Some schools had excellent math teachers or English teachers, while the next school had the opposite. I was intermittently confused when we moved to new schools. My deafness allowed me to learn to be self-sufficient.

As a young boy, mom would help me with everything. She folded my clothes, kept my room clean, and fixed us dinner every night. By the time I was in middle school my independence matured, and I wanted to do things on my own. I think in retrospect, she allowed me to venture out to do my own thing a little later than she would a normal child. Also, if I was allowed to make more mistakes, I probably wouldn't have made the big ones when I was an adult. We grew up in various homes. I counted that we moved over 30 times before I graduated college, and over 20 different cities.

Moving to a new place every few years seemed to add extra pressure on me. The same old routine – mom would tell each teacher I was deaf and they had to make extra sure that I understood everything, and on and on. Then I had to be a laughingstock for awhile. Then I might make new friends, or I was a loner. Like a broken record, I knew the routine. If mom wasn't there, she would remind me to always go to the front of the class. This practice continued all the way through medical school and even into my usual conference visits, I sit toward the front. I can hear with my new digital in the canal (IC) hearing aides, but it is much easier for me to follow them if I can see their faces too. I still utilize lip reading nowadays.

During play times, I was always alone despite the many invitations boldly yelped from a fellow boy in a clan or club. I was not ignorant but many thought so. Playing pickup basketball or volleyball never deterred me. Jumping into a game was easy. Always a speedster, defending well, and shooting outside promoted my "ignorant" status with the jocks all through middle school, junior high and high school.

When I moved from Stidham Oklahoma 4th grade to Oxford, Kansas 4th grade, I went from learning multiplication to learning fractions. It was schizophrenic in that way. Whenever memorization was required, I did well, but when improvisation was required, I did poorly.

Sometimes the teacher would have us come to the front of the class to discuss what we learned during the lecture. This always proved a problem for me as I never heard what was going on. I always wrote down the homework and learned on my own. When a teacher asked me about what we supposedly learned in English class, I couldn't tell her anything. I was profoundly humiliated in front of the class during those times.

When a teacher called on me to answer a question, everyone would look at me waiting for an answer. I always said the wrong thing. I thought the teacher would ask one thing, and I read her lips, but the answer I had always made students snicker and giggle.

Sweats and sheer panic attacks confounded me during some of the classes. I would try to control my breathing but nothing would settle me down. I would count down until the school bell rang and I could breathe normal again.

# Chapter 4

## The 50's Club

*Into The Dark*

*Whilst I ever be taken leave?*
*Or ever be left accompanied,*
*Or ever cherished by anyone,*
*By mom, father, daughter or son.*

*Whilst I ever be taken home,*
*Given comfort when agonies' gone?*
*Or do I have to go alone*
*To the dark where no light is shone?*

*Justus Peters MD*

I was often bullied and picked on to the point of isolation from any one group. Moving often allowed me to make some friends, but very few. Being the new kid in town, I had to start over frequently. My hearing had isolated me from the popular group, and I was without a core group of friends until I moved to Oxford, Kansas.

It wasn't very difficult to make friends, but my hearing deficiency had a lot of explaining to do. I grew weary of the many explanations. But this one group of boys in Oxford Kansas changed the status quo. Oxford was a small town south of Wichita about 30 miles, and north of the Oklahoma border about 30 miles.

My neighbor at our first house was about a mile down the country road. His name was Brandon Paris. Another friend I remember so well was Christopher Middleton, a direct descendant of a Declaration of Independence signer. These 2 guys along with a city boy, Bobby Welty and I became "The 50s Club."

We dressed up in the 50s. We had shirts that were small and we rolled up our sleeves and slicked our hair. We listened to 50s music all the time. Going to Wal-Mart, the only mission was to find old 50s radio station broadcasts with all the great songs.

I enjoyed Buddy Holly, Richie Valens, Big Bopper, Beach Boys, Chuck Berry. We shared our little tapes that were made from actual recordings of radio shows in the 1950s. I remember so many of the commercials. The Buick was described as, "magnificence unlimited." The Old Spice commercial song was sang by a pirate like voice.

*Yo-ho! Yo-Ho!*

*Brushless or lather boys,*
*Whichever you've a notion*
*Fifty cents for the shaving cream,*
*A dollar for the lotion.*
*„Old Spice means quality,"*
*Said the Captain to the Bosun.*
*Asks for the package with*
*The ship that sails the ocean.*

*Yo-ho!, Yo-Ho!.*

Brandon was "Buddy," I was "Richie," Chris was "Eddie," and Bobby was "Louie." We listened to classic rock and had our favorite bands. In fact when Bobby decided he liked a Bon Jovi song, we gasped. I smile when I think of that. I love Bon Jovi now and to think that he was a traitor to our group back then was so petty. I admire him for stepping forward and standing up for himself against our group.

I remember in junior high school one of the students told a group of kids that I breathe very loudly. I didn't know that I breathe loudly. I remember very clearly he impersonated Darth Vader about my breathing in class. After that I had a sensitivity to people hearing my breathing. I would then try to regulate my breathing in class so no one could hear it. I couldn't hear myself, so I didn't know how loud I was breathing. I would then be in the front of the class, and concentrate not on the lesson, not on the teacher, but on my breathing. That was how sensitive I was. I felt that if one breath would be loud, then all eyes would bore into my back. Every period seemed like a trial in anxiety control. I was bullied by older kids all the time.

I remember a tall lanky high schooler picking on a group of younger kids. At the time, I was reading Louis L'amour. One thing about L'Amour novels, is you learn how to talk back to someone who is bullying you. I puffed myself up and told him defiantly to run after me if he dare so and fight like a man. He ran upon me as fast as he could, and I dropped and twirled my legs, tripping him down the hill. He couldn't believe he just got whupped by a smaller junior high kid. All the kids and I ran away as he seethed with anger.

Even younger kids picked on me about my hearing. If younger kids were bullying me, something was wrong with that picture. Looking back I could see how someone might think of me as a "mute." I was even picked on by younger students about my hearing.

When I was an 8th grader, a 7th grader pointed to both his ears and screamed at me in his prepubescent screech, "You can't hear me? I can't hear you, I can't hear you!!! I'm deaf! I'm deaf! I'm deaf!"

What I did to him earned me a trip to the principle's office and date with the "spanker" board. Mr. Parks told my mom, what I done although understandable, was not right. Mr. Dallas never picked on me again though. I credit Louis L'Amour for all my back talking ways.

# Chapter 5

## Late Night Mentals and the Dark Clouds of Solitude

*Solitude, though it may be silent as light, is like light, the mightiest of agencies; for solitude is essential to man. All men come into this world alone and leave it alone.*

Thomas de Quincey (1785-1859)
British author and intellectual

I paid the ultimate penalty for putting my own hearing aides in the wash, by buying my own hearing aides after graduation. It was a pretty penny and I saved up for them by working at McDonalds every weekend during my junior and senior years of high school.

When I received my hearing aides for the first time in 11 years, I was awestruck. Sounds I haven't heard such as birds singing, and wind blowing through trees. I heard water as it hit the sink for first time ever. I couldn't believe how much I missed out.  I could even hear things without looking at them!

Hearing impairment can be quite fun, albeit trying. I have been a long time without hearing aides — since middle school. They are embarrassing to wear — like having bulbous lesions on your face. Sometimes I felt like the elephant man but with massive ears — that I wished enabled me to fly away like that pudgy gray circus animal Dumbo. What do people think of others who wear hearing aides? I have thought about it many times. Almost everytime I miss something that was stated, I think about it.

It was a quick sentence in the form of a question. I missed it, and the guys look at each other and smile. DAMN! I excuse myself, *"pardon me?"*

They repeat it but it still makes no sense. This is BS! It was like sitting there watching someone get kidnapped and there was nothing you could do. I literally would feel a cold knife pierce me in the chest, and I would strain to hear what was said.

I have seen the whisperings and the giggles from a distance. I have been more conscientious about my hearing in medical school than any other area.

I haven't worn a hearing aide since middle school. Hearing aides do anything but preserve the term "normalcy" to another human being. When an obvious deficit exists, the catalysis reaction occurs; first the person sees or hears a disability, then they form an opinion in their mind-this is a handicapped person- then they avert their gaze to dissuade any chance of conversation. Constant recurrences of this averted eye contact made me feel left out. When I would listen to someone, I always paid attention to anyone who was talking to me or whoever was talking in a group. They always had my undivided attention.

Millions upon millions of times this occurred to me, and the fulminant environment beckoned me to shyhood for the rest of my life. In fact, if it weren't for a junior high school student Steven Carter, who later became my best friend, I would still be shy. He brought me out of my shell. We spent every lunch hour together eating McDonald's and cruising mainstreet. It was a great way to spend your last semester in high school. I was grateful to experience the "popular crowd," that semester albeit shortlived.

What happened? I missed out on the here and now, today's best fashion designs-the hours of gossip that would have enabled me to be exhorbitantly anal. I spent the hours in my room learning the math, English, and writing skills necessary to succeed. I had to spend double sometimes triple the amount of time that others took to learn a subject. I read and reread, wrote and rewrote, and read some more.

I depended on my lip reading front-row seating in all my classes. It must have been pure luck that I did well in high school without hearing aides. Somehow I was ranked 9th out of 90 students at Eufaula high school when I graduated. Somehow, without hearing the teacher, nor the assignments, I copied the homework and taught myself a lot. There was hard work, but the experience of learning something new and getting good at it was very important. Studying vigorously wasn't a desire so much as it was a necessity. I was frantic to the point that I would be made fun of, or possibly jeered at.

I asked my mom once, *"What is a specialist?"* after reading the word in the paper.

*"A specialist is a person who is an expert in a certain field."* She replied.

Specializing in studying became my ultimate obsession. Persistence and perseverance were like two quiet guardian angels beckoning me onward. Studying was not only a way out, but also, a way to turn inward. To evaluate the most basic understanding of who I was and what I wanted to be was forged with studying.

Accepting hard work in class times, and in homework, reading entire lessons all developed my personality from within. What I couldn't hear from teachers or dissect what was discussed between colleagues in the same class was devoured after the last bell rang. Indirectly learning and teaching myself about everything possible, I persevered.

The dark clouds of confinement, of solitude, and solidarity were opened on that sunny afternoon in 1994. My new hearing aids were not completely "in-the-canal" hearing aids, and you could see them easily, but they didn't wrap around my earlobe like my old ones. The sudden sounds that hit me were both indescribable, and very memorable. Like a newborn baby thrust into the open air gasping for air, I experienced a multitude of sounds.

I can remember that day as if it were yesterday—very clearly. The light clouds over Muskogee softly soared, and the breeze was extraordinarily loud. In fact, I couldn't ever recall hearing the breeze before. The first new sound of the wind blowing by my ear was approximately like a normal person being put in a wind tunnel.

At 19 years of age and suddenly cast into a "new" world of hearing, it was hard for me to swallow. As the crisp wind whipped against my ears, I heard for the first time the chirping of birds. Birds were flying and singing, and tears flowed down my cheek. The sounds of the carwash a block away left me speechless.

With the suddenness of hearing clarity, I thought back on solitude and the questions. Yes, the questions....

Solitude can have a profound evilness to it that pervades the consciousness.

What might have been if I could hear perfectly? How might my personality differ? Would my downcast eyes and averted gaze continue throughout the day? Would the stage be a home? Would people think I ignored them all the time? Questions imbue my consciousness in extended moments. Was the reclusiveness my Hades? I couldn't stop thinking about the "what ifs."

After thinking about the wonders of sound, I wondered how I ever made it without hearing aids. How could I have been so dumb? This new life, albeit starting later in life, begins with newer possibilities on a new journey. A new journey could be fraught with potential injuries, but I was ready as I ever will be. Put in a new experience opened the door for me to desire new experiences regardless of potential risks.

These were not the risks associated with doing what my brother did, but were more global. My risk taking behavior went from nonexistent to normal. I felt I could do more than just be me in my own room studying. From the cave, into the world, I confidently walked.

Many people wonder what it is like to be hard-of-hearing. Think of the humming of an engine, or low pitched rumble of thunder. It is continuous-never ebbing, and monotone. When a car drove by, it sounds like low humming, when anyone talks, all I hear is a low hum.

In the 13 years of solitude and peaceful quiet, everywhere, everyone, and everything sounded the same. Every loud pop that shattered the still air on New Year's Eve, every scream during a scary movie, and every song that jumped from the radio elicited a low hum. It was truly a peaceful life I lived.

So on that new day, I could hear. The audiologist, a burly Harley Davidsonian grizzly man who stood over 6'3" and weighed over 200+ lbs. His Harley parked outside of the office right next to the entrance boldly reminded his customers about his hobby. He looked like he would visit Sturgis every year and give his office staff a vacation for 14 days in the last 2 weeks of August. A novel in itself, his character was full of vigor-a "man's man" with plenty of charisma. A medical John Wayne — he was brash, yet cheerful, opinionated and optimistic. I told him my dilemma. So he shared with me advice that helped down the road.

In my eyes, the obvious dilemma was being deaf in social settings. I couldn't hear with a lot of background noise. In the classroom, I had a lot of help with others writing notes for me, giving me tapes of the lectures, etc. With the new possibility of hearing closer to normal, I worried also about losing the peace and solitude that I have grown to embrace. Sharing some street smarts and experience with me, he smiled and said,

*"Get your education, get that knowledge and do what your heart wants. Do exactly what you desire to do. If you want to help someone, help them, if you want to act on stage, do so. If you want to be a lazy bum, be one. But I will guarantee this to you; no one can take away your education."*

I told him about emotional pangs of realizing other students' normalcy versus my impairment.

*"You are lucky,"* he consoled, *"you know what you have, and you treasure what you have left. You treasure what little left of your hearing besets in this little brain of yours."*

I rarely shared myself to anyone, and was called "stoic," and "incognito," more than once. I just thought I was a shy guy. But this burly man reassured me as my father hopefully would have if I was in a vulnerable position.

With that, I left that office and was suddenly cognizant of a new world of sounds. I drove to a car wash and couldn't believe what jet water sounded like when it came out in the spray and hit the car. The sweet birds' songs embellished my head with notes of such high pitch, I never fathomed. The sound of water trinkling from the faucet dropped my jaws in awe. I couldn't wash my face for awhile that first time. The clickety-clackety of traffic, people stirring, and voices talking adorned my sensitive ears. The nerve fibers bristled for the first time in my inner ear, and the memory storage banks filled up with new and exciting noises quickly.

What I missed since a young child was forgotten. What I verbalized during school was a remembrance of speech therapy class. What sounds my mouth elicited were now more than ever succinct. And I was aghast at my deficiency. I talked like I had cotton balls stuffed in my cheeks. Like the raspy Godfather, I couldn't say anything clear the first time. During the summer before my first year in college, I sometimes held my head in shame.

Since I acted with the drama club in high school, enjoying many plays and acts. I decided to go to North Carolina State University for undergraduate study.

# Chapter 6

## I was Roaming but now I'm Home

*The Crack in Life's Seam*

*On clouds of fire, I danced and sang,*
*To songs of dastardly love and thangs,*
*Acted with sore grace and raw thought,*
*Onto the stage I longed and sought,*
*For fulfillment of self esteem,*
*But found a crack in my life's seam.*
*No longer will I be or not to be,*
*Instead the greedy mare I see,*
*And lose the light I once had dreamed,*
*Thus crushed and hopeless I am deemed.*
*Until I hit the blackest bottom*
*Rummaging, rum, rum....*

Justus Peters MD

Although my first year major was biology or Pre-medicine, I enjoyed a different profession. The East Coast culture shock that ensued subsequently developed creativity in me. Having enjoyed drama in high school, I pursued Theatre Arts and Drama in my first year and acted in musicals and dramas with the Thompson Theatre.

My favorite musical was, "Anything Goes," where I learned to tap dance, sing, and act. They put me in the back line since I really couldn't tap. I did get a lot of dance education from the musicals I played in. Acting didn't seem hard, but it was fun.

The characters I played were multifarious as politician's personality. Characters included: a nerdy loser who misses a chance with the best looking girl in the school during a play; a preacher, sailor, and gentleman in a musical-for which I won the "Hammy" Award for Best Cameo appearance. A golden painted piggy bank adorned my shelf.

One of my fondest memories was performing in front of dad. He appeared surprised, entertained, and somewhat impressed with me. I am glad that I was put in the back row for the tapping routine. It was probably one of those moments every child wishes for—to be looked at with pride by their father--especially one who laughed at you when you missed a lay up in a basketball game.

My girlfriend and I were writing each other all the time. In Oklahoma, she was in her sophomore year, learning alongside my youngest sister, Becky. Becky was no doubt going through some of the things that I was going through in high school.

I was still scatterbrained during my first college year. Not thinking straight except for paying my bills on time, was all I could muster for the fast and frantic first semester of college. I didn't have time to complain much, except for my horrible tennis serve in morning physical education class. This could be due to the racquetball class that I took the hour before tennis, but I didn't know. My schedule was like clockwork.

I awoke at 0500 hours and ate my cereal, studied for 2 hours and then went to school. Classes lasted until 6 pm at night except on Wednesdays, and then I would head over to Thompson Theatre. We auditioned, and played, partied, and performed.

Part of the culture shock involved my first experience hanging around homosexuals. I was not a part of a lot of talk regarding the discrimination toward gays when I was growing up because I couldn't hear. I treated them as equals because I thought of myself personally as not as good. Having some inferior complex was a trial, and I constantly enjoyed any group or any one person's attention. The culture of college brought me out of my shell to say the least.

I enjoyed the parties, the early morning breakfasts, and the mayhem. While all the culture was fascinating me, I needed a second job by the second semester to help with my lifestyle. After the first semester, I had to make ends meet. I delved myself into school with a one paying job and a volunteer job, but it was a second job that introduced me into the field of medicine.

My weekend job with the local grocery store chain brought me enough to eat 4 sandwiches a day; 2 for lunch and 2 for dinner, and a bowl of cereal.  Needing a second job, I scrutinized the classifieds.

Easily obtaining a job as a nurse aid at the Cary Retirement Center, I worked every Saturday and Sunday morning from 0700 to 1500 (3 pm). The manager, Bill, was a gentle friendly man who encouraged me to get close to the residents. The nursing home was in an upscale part of town surrounded my trees atop a medium sized hill. An emotional bridge became a connection with patients, and the residents became my family.

The residents would see me come in every Saturday morning and wave at me smiling so brightly. I actually thought I was doing some good for a change. They called me by my first name and wanted me to come talk all the time. I felt like a superstar. I worked very hard for Bill and the Center, and enjoyed it. But where did the nursing motivation come from?

While working the nursing home, I observed every now and then a confident woman in scrubs would walk by with determination. The look upon heir faces stoic. I knew then I wanted to be a nurse. I saw them all the time. They were beautiful women who walked around handing out medicine. They looked very important and acted it as well. Their composure was always confident. Their backs rigid straight, and shoulders back. They smiled very rarely at me, but I always tried to get a rise out of them.

I wanted to be important, and being onstage didn't satisfy me as much as being a nurse aide. The "home away from home" was the Retirement Center, and I wanted to be someone. Being trusted enough to hold a dying patient's hand was empowering.

The first resident to die on me was one of my favorites. She was a large diabetic woman with huge glasses. Her heavyset belly never provided relief during our transfers from the bed to the chair to the wheelchair to the table to the wheelchair, and so forth. A great deal sweat was dealt in the personal care of her.

She took the most time for me to clean, to shower, and to feed. My back felt more pain after an hour with her than any other hour. But I loved her more because she was so helpless. I was gentle with her every minute. I cried when she died. I came in to help her and she was gone. Her hand so cold, yet strong I held to my cheek. In that brief moment my heart was set to dignify people who are helpless, to strengthen, and to heal those inflicted with pain and agony. I forgot her name, as it is somewhere deep in the memory banks. But I won't forget her.

I'll never forget taking care of a retired American Airlines pilot. He had models of 747s on his dresser. We had a routine everyday. With Parkinson's disease, he was slow to initiate most if not all of his motor skills. Pictures of Boeing 747s with American Airlines adorned his little room. The Captain's hat sat on his desk next to a plaque for great customer service. His brilliant motor skills reduced to a resting tremor, he steadied himself on the back of his recliner, while I bathed him. Everyday he repeated his ritual. Everyday, I washed him after breakfast.

Everyday, he waited for me and smiled when I greeted him. It wasn't just a calling to enter the field of nursing. It was an arduous climb up a mountain. Toiling through 10-15 showers per day to clean residents, running from dining room table to table to feed them, and transferring them from wheelchair to bed and back again for lunch all gave more than just sweat. It was a sense of accomplishment. If accomplishment was what I was after, I tried to find it in other ways then just nursing.

As a customer service clerk with Harris Teeter, I tried to always help the customer feel right at home. I did the job well, until I made a monumental brain fart.

One day a customer came in with a bunch of cash for a wire transfer. She told me about Equinox, and how she is making a bunch of money. Since I was working so hard, and making so little, I became tempted. She interested me and I decided to pursue.

It was one of the greatest mistakes of my life, to be momentarily dissuaded by something that seemed too good to be true. But I was young, and in retrospect, quite stupid. Even now, looking back, I find many instances where I failed miserably because of my hearing. I wouldn't hear the right line and thus trouble would ensue. I applied for a credit card with a limit of $300, and charged to go to a conference to learn the business of Equinox.

I was an idealist. This business involved a lot of legwork, and selling. This involvement eventually turned out to be a pyramid scheme. But I didn't know that. I dropped out of college and tried to make it in Oklahoma, specifically the small lake town of Eufaula. I know I left on a bad note with work, but that was the result of partying, not helping people.

I bought a car that I couldn't afford with mom co-signing a car loan. I spent a summer trying to build my own little business empire which was impossible.

I went door to door trying to sell some products that I believed in, but others didn't. I would spend the earnings at the local recreational facilities and mini golf. I failed miserably, and still have pangs of guilt for misleading the few people who believed in me and Equinox. One person, my barber, Diane, whom I admired and adored I feel like I stole her savings, and when I left town I left all their dreams to die.

I learned a lot from this experience. My dad allowed me to make mistakes after mistakes even as I was older. The older I got, the more expensive the mistakes were. I had to return my Eagle Talon I couldn't afford, and thus, my moms and my credit were destroyed. This was the legacy of Equinox, for all in one Summer, I lost my girlfriend, my car, and my business. I learned so much common sense, I decided to go back to school.

The anthem song for that summer was Roy Orbison's, "It's Over." I still remember the song on the rainy day I was kicked out of my girlfriend's house. The rain pelted my little car, and through some sort of ethereal osmosis, the tears from heaven became tears of my own. I still had so much to learn in this life. This wasn't just a major mistake to fail at a business, and steal someone's dreams, but it became a stepping stone in my infantile maturity of real life.

The feeling of hurting others was the catalyst to help them. Taking care of people was honorable and only a few wanted desperately to be one. This field of nursing was dignified and noble, and therefore I knew I would be a nurse.

# Chapter 7

## A Journey to Care

*Whatever Ails Your Aching Soul*

*A warmth, a kindness for you here*
*A soup, some bread, and loving care,*
*Whatever ails your aching soul,*
*Come unto me, I'll hold your bowl,*
*Let all your pains be shared with me,*
*I'll help you feel so light and free,*
*And when the end draws nearer still,*
*I'll still be here forever real.*

*Justus Peters MD*

Oklahoma requires certification to practice as a nurse aide, unlike Cary Retirement Center. I didn't take the course for certification instead I just took the test and practical at the local community college. I passed on the first try, and my certification arrived in the mail. That same day I drove to the hospital and presented it to Human Relations for a job. I became a certified nurse assistant in the summer of 1995. I didn't have to spend a dime.

No one told me I had to take the certification courses, and no one told me it was against the law to take the test without the course. I did the efficient thing to do because I wanted to do it now. Why pay over $500 for a course that you knew you already had the skills to do? On the job training at Cary Retirement Center was enough for me. The nurses taught me vital signs, correct transfer knowledge, and basic sanitation requirements.

Oklmulgee Memorial Hospital operated 3 floors with around 100 beds. The med-surg floor nurse manager interviewed me. She was a large woman. I would call her an "Amazon Woman." She was tall, not overweight. Her hair bodacious and blonde, hair sprayed up into a halo-like oval. Her glasses large and tinted maroon sat on a perfect nose between over-blushed cheeks, and pouty-Elvis lips. Her eyes were the most beautiful blue I had ever seen. Sometimes I can't remember if I wanted to become a nurse to make more money or to help people.

I told her of my work experience, gave her references, and spoke of my desire to help people. I really wanted to give her the impression that I cared deeply for my patients. I treated patients with the utmost of kindness, loving, and empathy. It was like I was destined to be a nurse. I enjoyed talking to the post-op TURP patients (transurethral resection of prostate.) I would talk to an ill elderly lady for hours. I cleaned each patient every morning with enthusiasm. It was such a pleasure to do the things that made both the patients and me happy.

My routine: vital signs done at 0700 for the nurses, bath and wash done after breakfast which was served and fed to invalids, and lunches too. In the afternoons I just answered room calls and became the scut-worker for the nurses. I enjoyed this job immensely.

I delved deeper into studies. I would go into work at 0500 hours to get patients' ready for surgery, transport them back and forth to surgery. I would also work on the floor as an aide. I would then go to classes for the day, and then work at night as a waiter. Work never fazed me. The more I worked the better I felt about myself. It was like, now that I could hear, a new life had opened itself up to me.

In the meantime, my sights were on getting an LPN degree (licensed practical nurse.) But my Aunt Deborah who had 30+ years of nursing experience, encouraged me to get my RN (registered nurse.) So I took all the prerequisites for nursing school at Oklahoma State University at Oklmulgee. I made straight A's in every class even with semesters with 20 or more credit hours. On top of that, I held a job at Okmulgee Memorial Hospital and Pizza Hut.

My hard work paid off, and I was inducted to Phi Theta Kappa, an honor society of two year colleges. My fun time was with the OSU drama club. The drama club was started by my current good friend Eric "Doc" Bay. Still awakening early every morning and studying every free moment, I was able to get the needed credits before nursing school started in the Fall of 1996.

*Diary entry July 28 1996:*

*Now this is what you call State of Emergency situation: Exam tomorrow and I am on Anatomy and Physiology cards. Pretty warm outside. Studied until deathly tired. Thought I was going to pass out. 6 patients today, I washed only 4!! Cool! Drama meeting was ok, my heart was slowing down. Studied from 5-11 and went to bed. Slept 5 hours.*

Being a nurse aide taught me how to treat someone as I wanted to be treated. When a patient is in the hospital, all kinds of fears, and emotions can make them worry. A nurse aide sometimes has to bathe, feed, and nurture the sick. A nurse aide did what nurses did back in the previous centuries. We did the menial tasks required to assist those who can't do activities of daily living. Those who can't feed themselves, we fed. Those who couldn't bathe themselves, we bathed. Those who couldn't walk, we assisted.

I learned that helping people at their most basic needs was rewarding. People with needs I could meet empowered me to focus on finding new ways to help.

# Chapter 8

## A Mirror that did not Reflect Me

*Tell me and I'll forget.*
*Show me, and I may not remember.*
*Involve me, and I'll understand.*

*Native American Saying*

So the summer of 1996 was a mirror image of the summer of 1995. From a colossal failure, to a burgeoning scholar, I was starting to find my calling. That summer, I attended OSU tech, Connors state college and Bacone College to fulfill requirements for nursing school.

In the summer of '95, I made a decision to leave a well respected college in a new car that I couldn't afford, and try to sell some health products, and failing horribly at that was hitting rock bottom for me. Falling for a pyramid scheme and hurting people was not what I wanted to do.

While I tried to be a successful salesperson, I learned it was very hard for my personality to overcome. Going door to door is not what I wanted to do. I didn't want to promise people riches and strike down their dreams. Still to this day I feel so guilty about that summer of 1995.

But the good thing that happened was the inner transformation of my soul. From the summer of 95 to the summer of 96, I trusted in more important things. I trusted in family, and the bonds with my siblings and mom were strengthened. I trusted in God, and prayed for wisdom. I trusted that I wouldn't make those dire mistakes again. I prayed that my naivete would mature.

My spirituality was always very strong. My mom raised me very close to the ways of the Bible. But I nearly came close to losing all hopes during that summer. Returning to Oklahoma the summer of 1995 was like going through the fire to reach bottom and realize that only I was truly in charge of my destiny. Now in this summer, I learned that outside of me mattered the most to other people. In the grand scheme, they cared for themselves. In my naivete, how could I think so much about what other people thought of me, and they not care?

As I heard more stories of what people say and go through, the more I realized my situation isn't really important in the grand scheme of things. People didn't really care that I couldn't hear. People really didn't pity you. If they did, they hid it well. It was enlightening to develop some sense of self in my early 20s. I imagine that if I could have learned this at an earlier age I wouldn't have been so sensitive. I feel that hurtful statements would have bounced off of me more easily. In retrospect, I finally learned that it didn't matter what people thought of me.

Hearing impairment's greatest damage was to my self esteem. Whether it was the inferior complex seeking acceptance from anyone, or the desire to be normal, I am not sure. I knew that I wanted more patient care. Through their ills and tribulations, I took comfort, because I felt what they felt. I knew what people who are suffering feel. I felt it everyday. My suffering was emotional and psychological. My only physical suffering came during football where I broke a bone every year I played in high school.

My patients' worries became my worries. Their fears became my fears. It never substituted my personal emotional turmoil, but instead it allowed me to deal with mine. Seeing people suffer is sad, but gives you reality in life. It makes you appreciate what you have. It makes you appreciate your own two feet, when you see a diabetic foot ulcer infected with gangrene. It makes you appreciate your eyes when you see a motor vehicle wreck patient brought into the ER with the side of his face missing. It makes you appreciate your hands when one comes in with traumatic amputation from a rope. Being a medical worker was therapy in that sense.

# Chapter 9

## Warriors of the Rainbow

*When the Earth is sick, the animals will be-*
*gin to disappear, when that happens,*
*The Warriors of the Rainbow will come to save them.*

*Chief Seattle*

The Bacone Billie R. Tower School of Nursing program sat on a plot of 160 acres of land in Muskogee, the "Indian Capital of the World." Professor Almon C. Bacone, a missionary teacher, started a school in the Cherokee Baptist Mission at Tahlequah, Indian Territory in 1880. Now called Bacone College, the annual enrollment was in the 400s. My mom went to school here and met my dad. They were both in the choir. My dad went on to become a Baptist preacher. My mom became an artist, writer and singer. My mom's parents went to Bacone, which made me a third generation student.

I knew in my heart of hearts that I could hear almost normal with my hearing aides, but I didn't have a special stethoscope or special hearing aides that allowed me to hear well. I said, "of course," without much confidence. I didn't want my disability to limit my horizon. I came this far to do good deeds. I made many mistakes and I wanted to do the right thing. I would learn more and more with my mistakes as I became a professional nurse and then a physician.

Living in a quiet world with a hearing problem made me appreciate what little hearing I did have. It made me sensitive to others who suffer. If you have hearing aides, I can totally understand whatever plight you personally had to deal with. If you have other disabilities, I can understand, but not as well. It doesn't matter what disabilities one has, they can overcome.

I was always a little paranoid. Because I grew up partially deaf, I became obsessed with how people viewed me. *"Did they know I can't hear? Or not?"* I was always looking behind me to see if anyone was talking to me. I would search people's faces to see if they were waiting on an answer from me. Constant searching became an obsession, which became a fear. I never became so paranoid that it was a psychiatric issue. Eventually I became afraid of confrontation, afraid of conversation. I delved deeper into my work, and kept my head in my studies.

The interview for nursing school by the Dean of Nursing was weird, and still sticks out in my memory. She was a large obese woman with a double chin and curly blonde hair overhanging brown eyes. Athough she was all serious, meant business, and was brutally honest, she had a gentleness to her that held behind a wall of roughness. Any 40+ year experienced nurse will have rough edges. The years of tribulations they had to take for the patients and the doctors will discourage any eager-eyed Pre-Nursing student.

After working in the field for a couple of years, I knew it was something my heart was set on. I didn't check the box that asked if I was hearing impaired, just like the many times before. Because I truly felt discriminated against when I checked hearing impaired, I would let the administration of whatever corporation, school, or person find out. It they brought it up quickly after seeing the hearing aids, I would realize that it is a frustrating issue, but they gave me good luck in future endeavors (no job included.)

Yet she asked, *"Do you have any disability that would require assistance?"*

"No." I replied.

*"You do not have any handicap that would disable you from performing a normal history and physical?"*

"No," I said again.

And then finally she asked, *"Do you have a disability that would disable you from keeping our patients safe from harm or wrongdoing."*

And I again said, *"No."* Did I lie? I did. I did so that I could break through the barrier of discrimination regardless of what the American Disabilities Act said. I wasn't going to get a lawyer to back me up if I didn't get into nursing school. I deserved the opportunity to help people without any thought of discrimination.

Her other questions simply asked about my life and why I want to be a nurse. She remarked that my experience of two years as a nurse aide was impressive. She was more impressed that I worked another job while in school.

Nursing school proved to be much harder than I thought. Learning Med Surg nursing, and Obstetrical nursing became a battle with sleep deprivation. My first experience with watching a baby being born turned me permanently away from ever wanting to be an Obstetrical nurse or doctor. The lady labored all morning long. The patient was about 250 lbs, and the baby was around 11 lbs. I was traumatized by the amount of bleeding that a woman had to go through with a delivery. The amount of screaming pierced my ears and reminded me again of the Halloween movies with Jamie Lee Curtis.

In 1997 during nursing school first year I was also in class for Organic Chemistry at another community college. In addition, I held a part-time job at the local hospital Muskogee Regional Medical Center as an Emergency Room tech.

In my diary, the days seemed to go by like a broken record. The usual day would start out with me waking up around 4 o'clock in the morning and going for run typically 3 to 5 miles a day and I would study and some reading I would then have to take a morning nap prior to school and so then going to lectures I would sit all day to lectures and then come back home and get ready for work. Typically I would do a couple hours of study with some friends who were female friends and we did well. A lot of my diary entries were very similar and the schedule showed consistency.

I'll talk about my grades on my test, or how many miles I ran in the day. Sometimes the weather or any major event is noted. If I went to the movies, I noted the titles. The major movies

I watched during nursing school were, *Get Shorty*, *The Rock*, and *The Titanic*. My common obsession was recording the number of miles I ran in the day and the total at the end of the week. I kept clippings from newspaper sports pages on the races I ran.

I enjoyed nursing school immensely, and next to medical school was probably the funnest years of my life. Socially, I was involved in activities encompassing 3 different counties, acting for a community college improv comedy group, learning nursing at a nursing school, and already working on pre-med classes in another college. I look back and can't see how it could have been better. I was involved in probably more than I could swallow. Instead of getting active in organizations, I could have focused more on the here and now, which included my education.

One diary entry reminded me I was scoring the top score in a Pathophysiology test, and the next week barely passing an exam. I even failed a couple exams in nursing school. Regardless of all the activities I put on my plate, it felt like a renaissance such that I didn't get to experience while in high school or junior high. I was inward thinking, introverted, and less sociable. Now I was excited, healthy, and enjoying life.

I was an Oklahoma/Arkansas Regional Vice President of Phi Theta Kappa, which enabled me to travel to Nashville and stay at the Grand Ole Opry Hotel, and to Bellingham Washington for the National Honor's Institute. I was fascinated by the politics involved and the representation required of me. It was like a big show. I was diplomatic and said very little, which at the time was opposite of what a politician was. Yet, the brief moments involved in running for big offices with the state and nation took me away from the focus of learning about nursing. In the end, it came to almost being dismissed from nursing school.

The Dean of Nursing called me to her office. Anxiety crushed my chest. Sweat beads formed in my deodorized armpits. My heart began to race. I always think about what is causing the anxiety first and foremost and try to minimize the issue. Minimizing is a defense mechanism everyone uses. It is normal and required to maintain sanity. Still I couldn't place what I did wrong to elicit a visit to the Dean's office.

*"Justus, we are looking at your reports here and we are disappointed."* She looked at me condescendingly.

*"What do you mean?"* I asked.

*"Why didn't you tell us that you were hearing impaired?"* She asked, although I think she knew the answer.

She obviously wanted to put me on my spot, and let me know that I broke the rules by lying on my application.

*"Is it an issue?"* I asked.

Either I was unaware that being hearing impaired was an issue or that she was using it to manipulate me. This could easily be done, as I was all about pleasing people. I never wanted to do anything wrong, and felt justly punished if I took one step off the beaten path. I felt like anyone at any time could wrench me away from my dreams. I felt powerless to defend myself, because any time my hearing became an issue, I felt inferior, and thus became too weak to do anything.

If it was an issue, why didn't they bring it up right after my first clinical experience? Everyone knew I had hearing aids. Why wait until I screw up somewhere and then come down on me? Policies screw people left and right. The policies of Banks, Insurance companies, and major corporations-all the fine print will jack us in the end.

*"Why did you just tell us that you were going to these two conferences without asking?"* She surprised me with this issue. I hadn't a clue why I did.

Sometimes I act without thinking and I know what needs to be done to get ahead in life. To me, going to these two conferences would enable me to network, to learn, and to help my education. One was the National Nurses Student Association National convention in Cleveland Ohio, and the other was in Nashville Tennessee with Phi Theta Kappa as an International President candidate.

I didn't see any reason not to be able to go to both conferences. I was doing well in school, or so I thought at the time. I was double majoring in Science, so I had to take other classes, and I still kept my job in the Emergency Room as a Patient Technician (professional for nurse aide.) The only thing that went through my head about what she could be talking about is some policy that I broke. Also in retrospect, I failed a test in community nursing, and was on probation.

*"We are looking at your clinical experiences and the staff reports you are falling."* She observed.

*"Why?"* Was it my hearing? Or did I breach protocol?

*"You know you aren't supposed to flush a nasogastric tube with cold water. Why did you ask to go out for lunch, when the policies clearly say no?"* Now there was a litany of issues that the administration had against me. I couldn't do anything really without having to answer for my actions.

*"What? That was sterile water, it was a mistake. My preceptor and I had already talked about that. And the lunch thing was purely a mistake. I didn't know."* I surrendered.

*"Well we are worried that you are getting ahead of yourself, and you need to focus on this educational experience. We can't let you go to both, and you can't walk around telling people that you are doing whatever you want. You need permission. With the way your clinicals are going,*

*you may not be able to go at all."* She left one eyebrow raised to nail down the "truth."

*"I am sorry. What do you want me to do?"* I was genuinely scared. I didn't know the real power of the Dean of Nursing until this day when she questioned my ability as a nurse. I thought I had to just shake my head and do whatever it takes to pass. She was using my clinical reports to scare me. The panic-mongering worked, and I succumbed to the pressure.

*"I will just go to one,"* I relented.

She softened a bit, happy that her power gave her success. *"We know that someday you will be something big, but we have to pull you back and make you realize that this is an important step for you. You must do well in school. You must take care of our patients".* She looked down at my portfolio and chuckled with heightened eyebrows.

*"Someday, you will be somebody, but for now, you are just a nursing student."*

Talk about killing butterflies. I began to count down the days to graduation after that incident. It is amazing how much politics is involved in professional schools, moreover, in private schools. I was the 3rd generation Turner to be a student at Bacone College, and I still was treated like a rotten egg.

This solidified my thought processes that others don't care about you, they care for what you do, and if you don't screw up. But if you screw up, they will squash you like a bug.

I was raised by a very loving mother, and I thought that caring about other people was noble and honorable. This was one of many confrontations that I had that hardened my heart. A small bump in my journey through life, and I start to develop street smarts.

# Chapter 10

## Buffalo Moon

*The American Indian is of the soil, whether it be the region of forests, plains, pueblos, or mesas. He fits into the landscape, for the hand that fashioned the continent also fashioned the man for his surroundings. He once grew as naturally as the wild sunflowers, he belongs just as the buffalo belonged...*

*Black Elk Oglala*
*Sioux Holy Man*

My first job outside of nursing school was working as a surgical nurse. Talk about challenging, I couldn't read lips well in the OR suite. Compounding that problem was the fact everyone wore face masks to cover their lips. I had a prolonged probation period, because I needed 3 chances to pass the Nursing Board exam. These were trying times for me. I was a hard worker, doing everything told of me to the best of my ability, to seem irreplaceable.

One time I completely had no hearing aides one day, and was stuck with orthopedic surgery and the nurse I was working with understood however. But I was so down on myself, I sometimes couldn't see straight. Despite how hard I was being on myself, other people seemed to be very understanding. I would get some "pity smile," from the boss almost every day. My self esteem plummeted. I was drawn to men to help me during the hard times.

I met a man named Randall Jenks. He was a CRNA at this hospital. With large square glasses on a round face framing an eternal 5 o'clock shadow, a cheesy wide grin, and light blue eyes, he was the best guy I ever met full of wit, ethics, and integrity. He was great with the patients, great with the staff, and especially kind to me. He served as a 1st Lieutenant in Vietnam, and was promoted to Captain in the Army reserves. He was proud to be the first male nurse in his nursing class, and fell in love with another nurse in the class. He told me how he wooed her to him.

Thinking of him brings many smiles to this day. He also was so proud of his son. You would have thought he was an executive for the rental company he worked at. He couldn't stop talking about how great his wife and daughter are as well. I enjoyed just being around such a great guy. He was so excited to be my best man for my upcoming wedding. I couldn't think of anyone else who could match how great I thought Randall was.

He met a couple of my girlfriends including Donnette before I proposed to her. Just as many things have hit me hard and proved to be mountains to climb, this one was the hardest of all. Randall unexpectedly died before he could make it to my wedding right before I graduated med school, but his "peace" plant lives on in my home, and his memory stays with me forever.

I remember when at the funeral, the family wanted it to be an open forum for all to share what they thought of Randy. I remember being nudged by Donnette, and standing up.

The tears flowed freely, but I started, *"Randall was the best man I have ever known. He was supposed..."* I paused, wiping some tears away.

*"He was supposed to be my best man."* I cried, and an audible sigh could be heard over the entire room. I wanted to say more for him, but everyone knew that what I said was enough.

Being a pallbearer was a great honor for Randall. I am forever indebted to the Jenks family for what this man did for me in those deep dark days during my nursing board test failures. When I told him, I had failed, he said, *"it's just a test, man, you got another shot."* He was always optimistic for me. He would always teach me to look at the silver lining. He was definitely a father figure at a time I needed it.

I remember my scariest ER moment back when I was a registered nurse. A 50-something white female rushed into the ER via EMS, was pale gasping for breath, and clammy. She was in severe respiratory distress. She didn't seem old enough to be having a heart attack, but back then as the nurse, I just cared about getting the little stuff done — stuff the doctor ordered.

Grabbing blood vials I placed an IV in her largest Antecubital vein on her left arm and drew up 5 vials of blood. We began running Normal Saline through it. The patient's Pulse Oximetry read 80% while on oxygen mask which was delivering 100% oxygen. Something was not right.

She clearly was not reacting to the oxygen. The respiratory technician drew an arterial blood gas on her and rushed to get results. The ER doctor was intensely listening to her chest. He was somewhat disturbed but still calm. I had no idea what it could be that was causing her problems.

Her heart rate was tachycardic, fast over 120 beats per minute. She was experiencing some Cardio-pulmonary dysfunction.

*"Breathe through the mask!"* I yelled. Holding her clammy hand, I squeezed it. Her eyes stay focused on the ceiling. Her light blue eyes searching passed through me and the ceiling into the sky. Her mouth wrought in agony.

Her sweat rolled off her temples, her hair plastered to her head. Her hair was dark gray.

The doctor strained for her breath sounds. I didn't know what he wanted to do.

*"That's it, take her to CT now!"* he screamed.

I called the Radiology department and we rolled her right out of the ER.

Her breathing continued at a harried pace — 32 breaths per minute. However, those respirations were not complete respirations — they were varied in tempo and volume. The doctor shouted out to get her Arterial Blood gas results.

The respiratory tech reported that her pH was low, which meant the patient was not getting rid of her $CO_2$, causing acid to produce, thus lowering the pH. Her $CO_2$ level was high, $O_2$ level was low. Instead of intubating her right then and there, she was wheeled into a room that was not ideal for a code.

My anxiety started rising. The doctor's pupils became dilated as the information sunk in. Our anxieties became matched. The doors to the CT room slammed open.

We placed her on the CT table. The CT was done in 5 minutes, but not before she reached respiratory failure. We called a Code right there on the CT table. She died after 30 minutes of unsuccessful Advanced Cardiac Life Support.

I remember utilizing as much of my nursing skills for all my patients. I utilized my empathy with the family which worked best. I have made mistakes in nursing as we all have. But we learned from that.

One time, in the ICU, I was watching over a patient that was cared for by an internist resident, and he had circulatory collapse. His blood pressure kept getting lower and lower. He had a severe infection what we call Sepsis, when the blood pressure becomes low, and the body starts to fail to compensate. I followed orders, as the intern increasingly began to worry.

I kept increasing his medicine to increase his blood pressure. The intern kept coming in and checking on things. He was worried, as the patient was complaining of chest pain. The problem with chest pain is that it is an ominous sign that a heart attack could be happening. The intern and I monitored him, and drew labs and checked him constantly.

He continued having worse pain, and he ended up developing a heart attack from the medicine. This can happen when you are trying to keep someone's blood pressure up. But it was devastating for the team, me and the family to fight so hard for someone so sick, and fail.

Guilt grows in the medical field like wildfire. At least I feel a certain amount of guilt with any mistake I make. No one is perfect, and yet, when it comes to the human body, the medical and nursing field feels incompetent if we let anyone die that we could have saved.

Sometimes the inevitable happens and everything is expected. One day a patient arrived to the Emergency room with upper gastrointestinal bleed, jaundice, and end stage liver disease with a very bad prognosis. In fact he came from hospice. When I was a nurse, I thought that if someone was in hospice and they come to the hospital, then they lose their spot with the hospice company. This is not true. In fact, a hospice patient can come to the hospital and stay with the same company regardless.

I thought that I had explained to the wife all the consequences of doing what the husband wanted. He was clear and cognizant when he said he wanted no intubation.

I received a call day 2 of admission that the wife didn't hear from anyone about the options.

She repeatedly told us that her husband had wished not to ever get intubated again.

He told me that he would never want that kind of pain again. He said yes to blood but no to intubation. It was decided that there would be no heroic measures taken.

Over night his condition worsened. We gave him 2 units of blood, but he decompensated. He developed confusion and altered mental status, thus what we call "encephalopathic."

In a liver failure patient, when the brain begins to die from lack of oxygen or blood or with too much ammonia, then they develop hepatic encephalopathy. He wasn't responding to verbal name calling and everything else. He would try to open his eyes, but nothing was coming out of it.

This gentleman was the most yellow I have ever seen. His sclerae were dark yellow. His bilirubin was 33.3. The bilirubin is produced in the liver, and if the liver is cirrhotic or so diseased, the bilirubin just absorbs into the vascular system depositing all over the body thus giving it that yellow color. Bilirubin is the chemical that makes our bowel movements brown, green or yellow.

Sometimes, you are the only one that cares. One time, I was taking care of a man post op arterial bypass graft from his femoral artery to his popliteal artery (fem-pop bypass). He started complaining that his toes were getting numb.

I did an assessment, and called the doctor on call, who didn't order anything to be done. I then called the patient's doctor who told me to call the surgeon. After those two calls, I made the mistake of not calling the surgeon, because the patient reported his symptoms were gone and he felt fine. I worked very hard for him that night, but received a censure from the Nebraska State Board of nursing.

It was another mistake I had, which was not lawyering up. That censure really was a slap on my face, when it should have been a slap in the doctor's face.

# Chapter 11

## Med School Miracle

*To suffering there is a limit; to fearing, none.*

*Sir Francis Bacon, Essays (1625),*
*"Of Seditions and Troubles"*

I have applied to several medical schools, and have been denied acceptance for 2 straight years. My Medical College Admission Test scores were too low. The MCAT tested basic and advanced sciences such as physics and organic chemistry. A writing test was also part of the MCAT, and my first essay was one of the highest percentiles in the nation, but my science scores were awful.

I was a counselor for the National Native American Youth Initiative and spent a week in Washington D.C. This proved to be a turning point that connected me with a couple of potential medical schools that would take me. The University of Oklahoma and Creighton University had multicultural departments aggressively recruiting Native Americans for medical school.

I went through a Kaplan Review Course and improved my score but not enough through the second round of applications. I was getting discouraged about the entire medical school journey, until one day I received a call from Creighton University Post-baccalaureate program.

This program was a year-long intense study in all the facets of sciences, English, and writing. This class was basically an open opportunity to succeed at the MCAT and thus be given a chance in medical school at Creighton University.

I was working in the cardiopulmonary floor where patients go after getting stents or for rule out coronary syndromes, when the call came. I was accepted to the program, and my heart hit the ceiling. The rest of my shift flew by, and it seemed that no bad news could kill my butterflies.

After that, I daydreamed about the move up to Omaha, Nebraska to that little private Jesuit College. Finally, my mom and sister helped me with the move and we drove all the way from Tulsa, 8 hours away.

The program year was intense and every day we were put through multiple different lectures in all the sciences, and English, and writing. This class was the inaugural class of the post-bac program after it was disbanded back in the 8os. A lot of pressure could be felt as we were trying to do well not just for ourselves, but also for the program. Dr. Wilson, the School of Medicine Dean brought on a champion Dr. Kosoko-Lasaki to lead the Post-Baccalaureate program.

Dr. Kosoko-Lasaki was like a mother to me. She always encouraged me during that year, and even during the 4 years of medical school, I learned so much from her. She was the multicultural affairs director, and was still practicing ophthalmology.

I believe it was a success story in and of itself, that Dr. Wilson revived the program, and that the first bunch of us, miraculously got into the next year's class in medical school. If I failed

at anything more in life, at least I knew I got in
to medical school, and that was a major miracle.

# Chapter 12

## Taking an Oath

*Cancer Sonnet*

*Breathing entity before me so still,*
*Awaiting of what I despaired to see,*
*My heart in pain so deep and hurt I feel,*
*To tell her the diagnosis would be,*
*Before me lies a loving living scene,*
*With memories of her I just wonder,*
*Her life stories of past and future seem*
*Of what future therapy lies yonder,*
*Of funny times with families and friends,*
*Of spoken words, conversations and thoughts.*
*From here a journey for her I will send,*
*This moment a speck of time I have got,*
*With this woman so precious a sweet friend.*
*My patient's wet eyes away my answer,*
*With my hands on her hands, "you have cancer."*

*Justus Peters MD*
*11/19/09*

Sitting in my room one day I looked up at the large framed piece of art, my mother in law made for me. It was a beautiful rendition of an Old English style font, with large colorful drawings and paintings of different anatomical structures, including the vertebral spinal column, pelvis, a shoulder girdle, and an intrauterine fetus. She had burned the edges of the page to give it the "aged" look. The Hippocratic Oath was painted in the old style writing and I began to read the first paragraph.

*"I swear by Apollo, the Physician, Asclepius, Hygieia, and Panacea and all the gods as wells as goddesses, to keep according to my ability and my judgement, the following Oath and agreement:"*

I wondered as I read the oath who and what those gods were. Why did these names have a place in our oath? I learned that the goddess Febris, could cause and cure fevers. The Hindi goddess, Sittala, did the same. Apollo was bringer and reliever of plagues as depicted in the Iliad. The goddess Hygieia, the daughter of Asclepius, was the guardian of health or disease prevention, and Panacea, the goddess of healing.

I remember reciting those words at the White coat Ceremony at the beginning of the medical school freshman year. It was revolutionary when it was written 2500 years ago, but I didn't know. I had no idea how it related to modern medicine and its practice. Prior to this time, doctors and magicians were practitioners of the same science. William Osler wrote in "Evolution of Medicine," that magicians and sorcerors were the only ones to cure disease, while doctors treated symptoms.

The Oath was the first of its kind to separate humanistic medicine and the practice of the inhumane. It is an oath worth repeating and remembering as trusted professionals serving the public because we care. My mom told me when I decided to become a physician that I would always be a public servant.

The teachers pave the many trails of education. Directly proportional to the time they spend teaching is the success of the student. Most teachers I hope still believe in what they do. When I read the 2nd paragraph, to understand it clearly, I understand more importantly the value of the Art of Medicine. During the years of medical school, internship, and residency, I respected those who taught me. They have given me their time and energy, and thus invested in me trust for the common people.

Considered an art long ago, now an advanced science, Medicine has now become so ubiquitous as to be a part of government intervention. The United States government now invests nearly 4 billion dollars into Cancer research alone. The medical community is truly blessed to be able to research newer ways to assist in treating patients. None of this would be possible without our many professors of medicine. Hippocrates saw this as an art however, back in the ancient times. The second paragraph divulges into the arena of those who taught the art.

*"To consider dear to me, as my parents, him who taught me this art; to live in common with him and, if necessary, to share my goods with him; To look upon his children as my own brothers, to teach them this art."*

Nowadays in med school we are taught all of the science of medicine. We learn the mundane details down to the chemical reaction between the molecules in all physiological pathways. We learn the various organic structures in pharmacology. But we forget sometimes about the Art of Medicine.

Hippocrates reasons that the bonds of our fellow colleagues include an understanding of what Medicine really is. While the scientific method wasn't constructed until way after Hippocrates wrote his treatise, the basis of most science started with an Art. Early astrologers painted stars before they realized that a mathematical construct could predict when stars would be in certain points in the sky. Early inventors practiced many voluminous drawings of possible technology prior to creation of the machinations detailed by scientific knowledge.

My professors taught ethics in Medicine, the principle of beneficence, and self-autonomy. Directly corresponding to a Constitutional right to life, liberty, and pursuit of happiness, medi-

cal ethics opened our eyes. The professors themselves were varied in style in personalities, and
color. I learned a lot from few and a little from a
lot, but I always respected them as the expert. I
depended on every word they said.

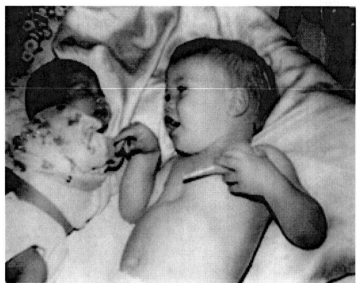

*Infant Elizabeth and me.*

*The Peters family 1981-1982*

*My first family portrait, Roo, Dad, Ma, and me.*

*This is basically my childhood in a picture. Elizabeth has her "bankie," Becky and I are hanging out, and Roo doing something creative.*

*The 50s gang, Brandon "Louie," me "Huey", Bobby "Frankie," and Chris, "Eddie."*

*One of the many days of studying*

Becky and I before going to med school.

The author, Dr. Sade Kosoko Lasaki, and my roommate Eddie Moran

*Finally in practice! First white coat as Intern*

*In a village in Palestine taking care of elderly*

Jonathan McRay, me, and Dr. David McRay at the Valentine Hotel in Petra, Jordan.

Monastery at top of Petra, aka Al-Aydr

*Peters Family today*

# Chapter 13

## The Journey of Medical School

### A Journey

*She fills my waking moments,*
*With sweet honey tasting cherish.*
*She finds my heart with love,*
*As wide as the seas above.*
*She goes further for me,*
*Than endless eternity.*
*She makes my world go round,*
*Than any being ever found.*
*She gives me whole heartedly,*
*Her blessings to infinity.*
*She heals my lasting heart,*
*That from her I could never part.*
*She loves me endlessly,*
*As if today was the end of me.*
*She touches ever so soft,*
*To send my heart aloft,*
*She brings me soul to feed,*
*My desires, wants, and needs.*
*She hopes, and laughs, and cries,*
*In times of love by and by.*
*She longs for me each day,*
*And loves anew in her sweet way.*
*She learns unselfishly,*
*And teaches the pride in me.*
*She sees me dear and strong,*
*For me she eternally longs.*
*She loves me and loves me,*
*So much it hurts thee,*
*And all I need is her,*
*To cherish and love forever,*
*And happiness I found to be,*
*The love of Donnete for me.*

Justus Peters, 2003

Anatomy 101

Every first year medical student experiences the Gross Anatomy Lab which provides the most memorable experience. Experiencing morning lectures from 0700 to 1100 hours and then afternoon anatomy lab hours provides the medical student the knowledge of the most basic science; the never changing anatomy. Each crevice, bump, and notch is a factual name in the medical text. Each layer of skin is documented, and each cell that pervades the system has a name.

Total immersion into this most basic of sciences provides what I can only describe as a time warp. The moment I stepped into the Anatomy lab, I watched people everyday with a blur. I felt like if Einstein could study me surrounded by a blur, I would be evidence on the theory of relativity. Each moment seemed like both an eternity, and a blink of time. Each step was a mile and a millimeter.

The only scientific class that doesn't have a continuous changing dilemma is Anatomy. Of course we learned that medicine isn't an exact science, and our bodies react to medicines differently perhaps, but not restricted to genetic make-up. However, the anatomy of the human body is essentially the same as it was 200 years ago when morticians sold bodies for science, and over 400 years ago when Leonardo Da Vinci sketched organ parts and pathophysiology in the name of art. Nevertheless, Anatomy continues to be researched to improve the wonderful world of science.

My personal experience is "Esther," an 86 year-old frail woman who I owe my thanks for such a wonderful semester of learning. My team worked with her learning of the reality of life and death. A human body, lifeless-yet full of life; soulless-yet beheld memories of happiness, sadness or betrayal perhaps, and most importantly love.

The human body is the most brilliant demonstration of science. Esther, in all her magnificent glory displayed within her vessels, heart, lungs, and brain, epitomized the transformation of me into a scientist and moreover a future physician. Over the course of the semester our trying minds researched our findings on this woman and learned of what ills she beheld in her final days.

Survival of medical school is mostly time management and attitude, I learned. Anyone can have a set of abilities to get through. The reason I believe my advice is better is that I was able to do so much more. I trained every morning for marathon running, wrote diary entries, read novels and enjoyed myself through the first semester. I even kept a part time job with a nurse agency.

Most medical students immerse themselves in the medical books all afternoon. Because I awoke at 0400 hours every morning, I was able to have solid scheduling for studying. Many questioned how I was able to get up so early. It wasn't hard for me. An alarm clock always wakes me up. I guess it would be more difficult for someone who can hear normally to wake up to music. I would be able to jump out of bed as soon as the alarm clock erupted with rock n' roll.

While in med school I contributed a couple articles for the Wellness Chronicle. One of the articles I wrote involved time management. Of course, time management for the medical student is helpful for other professions as well. Even if someone doesn't have a job, they could improve their time management with tips.

When I walked into the Anatomy lab every morning at 0500 hours, it was cold and lonely. I was always there alone. No one in my class save for my roommate Eddie, who I would drag out of bed every now and then, would come with me and work on our dissections.

Waking up early is a beautiful thing. It is the sound of darkness, the peace and tranquility that permeates the air that refreshes me. The stillness of the streets brings a smile to my face whenever I drive. The early morning highly caffeinated Red Bulls always helped me stay awake and alert through the morning rituals.

For 2 hours, I would toil with "Esther," and learn the beauty of every important organ, bone, muscle, and fiber. It helped in the end when I

was able to score in the highest percentile during the actual lab exams. I wouldn't only work on
"Esther," I would also spend time on other bodies to learn of the different anatomical versions
of a certain ligament or muscle attachment. This
helped tremendously during the lab exams.

*October 21, 2001 diary entry:*

*"I woke up this morning at 0400 again and ran for
6 miles in a nice quiet morn. It was a very cloudy, foggy
morning; my favorite. I enjoy this tremendously because
my anxieties are minimal when trying to breathe for more
than 45 minutes. I can smell myself reek of formaldehyde
or whatever that Lab smell is. My girlfriend said my car
stinks. I don't care, because my main thing is the anatomy
test coming up. It is over the Back and Brachial Plexus (set
of nerves running from the cervical spinal cord through the
arms.)*

*It is such painful agony figuring the projection of
the medial and lateral cord, and the muscles innervated by
the Ulnar nerve, and the travels of the Median nerve. If this
injury happens, what is the presentation? Blah blah blah!
Did you know that the medial border of the Pectoralis Mi-
nor muscle consists of the branch of the Subclavian artery
that perfuses the glands that cause you to have underarm
odor? What a coincidence!*

*I get depressed during the week before exams, not
because of the looming exam, but because fear of the unknown. I have to kneel every night before I sleep and cringe
and beg for the knowledge to remain in my head for the
exam. I have to humble myself each morning and continue*

*to run even when I would rather study the sketches, and work on "Esther." Tonight, I will again confront my fears of the unknown and relax for it is only a test."*

I think others thought I might have been crazy or something. They may have thought I was "the gunner." I had no intention of being the gunner. I trained for marathons and an Ironman but I never did great in medical school.

*"I don't know how you do it man."* One would say.

*"Man, you are crazy, You run at what time in the morning?"* was a good one.

*"How can you stay up during the day?"* one questioned.

*October 22, 2001 diary entry:*

*Today was my birthday and I always run on my birthday harder or so I think than the year before. It proves that I am not really "getting older." But I did, and went to anatomy lab at the break of dawn around 0530 after doing morning pushups and sit-ups. I am doing something I have not done in forever, which is keep a prayer journal. But it isn't really praying, it is writing down prayers that I think are very pretty. Most of it is good advice, too. Anyway, we have a small quiz today and I have already studied up a storm for this thing. It is over the back muscles and the thorax. I don't think I could have sat for another minute at Barnes and Nobles Bookstore because I was so tired.*

*Eddie gave me a cool tie pin which had the letter, "P" on it. Surprised me that he even could spell my last name! I also had note-service, which sucks. I could think of a thousand things to do besides note-service on my birthday! My girlfriend, Donnette, came by and we went to Old Chicago, which has good pizza. My friends all showed up. I had a couple of bud lights on tap and felt the slight buzz before heading home. Wow, what a day. I am so tired.*

I was a quiet student. My team was a very outgoing group so I learned a lot as they talked about certain parts of the body during the afternoons. The afternoon lab sessions would go from 1:00 pm to 5:00 pm most days, but we could stay up into the evening to learn more. Instead of staying at the lab, I would go to the library and check out the medical books to save money. The only book I paid for that semester was a Robbin's Pathology pocket book. I just spent the $500 on an electronic Littman stethoscope that enabled me to hear so much better the high decibel pitches of heart murmurs, and that soaked up most of my cereal money. I wasn't about to pay for medical books that I would be selling in a few years.

In the afternoon labs, the students would mostly be weary eyed and tired if they had a large lunch. The energy of the lab would carry us through into the two hours, and then we would feel the weariness later. Unless, someone was on Vivarin, or a caffeine pill, or Ephedra, then we were ready for naps. One of the cons of waking up early is that you have to take naps for your "second wind."

*"I am so tired that I could pass out right onto Esther right now."* I said one day.

In fact one day I was bent over Esther trying to locate her splenic artery and my weariness came upon me and my nose bounced off her liver for a second. I quickly regained consciousness.

*"Justus, did you just plant your face in her liver?"* someone asked, looking at me concerned.

*"I don't know, man I just need to take a nap."* I retorted.

My friend who was as much of an anatomy lover as I was who I will call Eric, always stayed late with me and would study with me each day. He was laid back, scruffy, and had a mellow outlook on life. I was always at ease around him. He would have this funny laugh that sounded like he was on the toilet.

Juggling medical school with a relationship was difficult in the least and tenuous at best. I couldn't just break up with someone. I had to gently remove myself away as best I could. Long distant relationships didn't work for me. So during medical school, I met Donnette, my future wife. We started out as running partners, and then we became friends while eating at the local Village Inn. Soon thereafter, we started dating. She was different than what I have experienced with before. She was strong willed, Type A

Personality, and a perfectionist. She was a talker, and I was a listener so it naturally worked out.

A recurring theme in med school was that I would not hear the question that was asked, and follow it with a wrong answer. I felt the stares, every second on them. Whether they were stares of disdain or disappointment, I didn't know. What they caused were shame and humiliation. I cannot count the number of times I felt like I should stick my head underground like in the cartoons.

In one of my diary entries, I obviously took offense to some of the heckling by students. Professors will sometimes ask students questions during class. The class is a large auditorium, which didn't help the hearing aids. The diary entry:

I hate it when those crazy students laugh when I say something wrong. Do you think I am mumbling?

Of course, I knew why they laughed. And it wasn't my mumbling thick lisp. I answered inappropriately. It was a common theme for me to answer questions inappropriately. It was embarrassing, and I still have some issues with it, but Donnette has helped me embrace my deafness by making it fun.

If I hear the wrong thing, I repeat to her what I thought I heard, and she cracks up. A sentence or a question will have no relation to what I thought was said.

*"Do you want me to cheer the vases on?"* I would look at her quizzically.

*"No! Do you have your hearing aids on?!!"* She retorted, rolling her eyes.

# Chapter 14

## Medical School Survival Guide

*Disappointment to a noble soul is what cold water is to burning metal; it stengthens, tempers, intensifies, but never destroys it.*

*Eliza Tabor*

If you make it to medical school, a few things have helped me survive, if not succeed. I wasn't an over-the-top smart guy, but I was resourceful, and utilized every possible one to get by. The most important thing to do is to stay healthy. If you missed a week of medical school, you might have to retake the whole year. It truly felt like survival of the fittest.

Here is a list:

- Hydration begets blood volume begets healthy heart begets oxygenated brain. Drink water, juice, milk-skip the soda, caffeine decreases blood volume by making you urinate more.

- Increase heart rate for 30 minutes with any activity-walking, swimming, running, and whatever-unassisted with Ephedra or Sudafed, of course.

- Keep a log; if you awake at 0600 hours and start doing push-ups or sit-ups. Write numbers and exceed these with increasing endurance and strength. Keeping a log increases motivation.

- Utilize resources-surrounded by doctors? Get a mentor-write a letter to them introducing yourself and get their advice on your health. I had a mentor Dr. Condrin who never hesitated to give me advice on my health as well as medical knowledge.

- High Protein, low carbs= more concentration. Everytime I had a high carb snack,

I would fall asleep from post meal sugar flush during lecture. But when I had an EAS low carb (2g) high protein (13g) French vanilla drink, in mid-morning lectures, it carried me through to lunchtime where...

- Keep lunch light. Once again, heavy lunch will crash you in the afternoon lectures or study times.

- Morning breakfast is MOST IMPORTANT meal. A 50/50 protein and carbohydrate meal helps. You need the sugar to think, also because you are hypoglycemic from 6-8 hours after sleeping. The protein helps consolidate your carbs.

- Maintain a relationship....with somebody, everybody, including family. It can be your priest, best friend, mother, brother, anyone you can trust to listen to you complain. Abraham Lincoln talked to a friend for 6 hours about slavery and Emancipation before he bid him farewell. His friend didn't say a word. Abraham needed a friend to listen, and then he proclaimed the famous "Emancipation Proclamation."

- Have fun. These 4 years will be the best years of your life and I promise they will fly by quickly. Four years is a long time and important. They will help you grow emotionally and mentally.

- Keep your mind on the "Big Picture." The easiest way I could calm down was to constantly remind myself that it would soon be over and I would be an M.D.

- Always take time to replenish yourself. Every man, woman, and child should take some personal rest and relaxation each day. Every minute we grow older, and every hour we draw nearer to our demise.

Why should we exclude ourselves from the indulgence of happiness? Whatever the indulgence of the individual, whether it be movie watching, television, music, calling friends, or eating, we should then satisfy it during a designated time.

One of my colleagues always watched "Friends" reruns every night at 7:00 pm before taking back off to school to read more. I loved to read. I would read a chapter at a time of my favorite novelists such as, Tom Clancy, Dean Koontz, and Lawrence Sanders.

I would be reading 3 novels at a time. If I sat on the toilet I had a novel, if I needed to rest my eyes from medical lingo, I had a novel for fun. Reading brought me to a fantasy world away from the realism and eclectic life of med school.

My roommate, Eddie Moran would play something on the Playstation, or computer. He is a fiery personality with a Type A persona. He could really burn into the books when he wanted, and it usually came the week before an exam. But his "R n R" occurred daily, and he was a happy man, and no one can take that away from him.

# Chapter 15
## Pediatric Rotation

*The Elephant in Your Ear*

*Parents' pride and joy unsure of me,*
*At first, a white lab coat, big smile,*
*Elevated brown sharing innocence, I see*
*Your eyes try to think while*
*I hear your mothers' heart*
*And look into her ear, you just stare*
*From her you glare at me again and bare*
*A questioned look such sweet curiosity*
*Unknowing of discomfort, or of pain*
*Let me in to see as close as I can be,*
*Turn your head and let me obtain*
*What parents' often always hear*
*Is there an elephant in your ear?*

*Justus Peters MD*
*5/07/2009*

My experience through medical school could take up an entire book, so I am really paraphrasing my experiences through it. Pediatrics was one of the rotations where I had a positive experience worth mentioning, primarily because my clinical preceptor, Dr. John Vann was simply awesome.

*Diary entry:*

*Up at 0400 again, went to lobby of Criss III and studied for the pediatrics shelf exam. The early janitorial staff greeted me again.*

*"Buenos Dia," (good morning) greeted the tall Hispanic man.*

*"Goodmorning my friend," I replied. A big smile illuminated our shared faces.*

I began to brainstorm a better and quicker way the share the medical knowledge. Sure there were plenty of authors out there, but I wanted to write stories that had a bit of trueness, a memoir-a newsletter or website of Resident's life. Medical Resident's Life. Editor or Editor-in-chief. A forum for the public-students-interested in medicine. Need to add AMSA and AMA-MSS to Resume.

Afternoon lecture called Medical Professionalism

Changing times gave us a reminder of what we are doing, and the greatness of the profession. To increase value of knowledge and skills in MDs. We had a Doctor who taught Creighton for 44 years and he talked too long. We had just taken a 2 hour test that a lot of us woke up very early for. The more I look at the more heads I see lower into the angle of their arms to catch a few winks of sleep. Dr. Egan put a few of us to sleep. A lot of students decided that it'd be best to just let him go rather than ask questions. I bet the transcript of his speech was over 50 pages, but in big print, for his age. I drew a revolver with a caption, *"Just Shoot Me!"* and showed it to my table which elicited a few giggles.

Dr John Vann is Jewish raised, married a catholic nurse, and graduated from West Side High School in Omaha, Nebraska. He got a B.A. at University of Nebraska, and MD at University of Nebraska Medical School (UNMC), and did his pediatric residency in Syracuse, New York. He is a proud father of 2 children, a son and daughter, as well as a foster child.

First of all, he was brutally honest about his views, and reminded me of the neurotic Woody Allen. His first priority was his children, which was honorable. He partnered with parents to decide the best care for the patient.

Like me, he treasured his nurses-and treated them with respect. He quizzed me though and enjoyed my despair after wrong answers to his clinical scenario question.

Beaming with pride he would say, *"What is it Dr. Peters, Orthopedic Surgeon?"* He called me orthopedic surgeon because at the time, I was dead set on going into orthopedics. He would always chime in,

*"What is the diagnosis Mr. Ortho Surgeon?"*

*"What would you present Mr. Doctor?"*

Colorful toe socks that he could quickly show his patients were surely an eye opener, but it put children at ease. His round head framed with thinning curly hair makes him stand out in a crowd. His clear blue eyes, broad forehead, and clownish smile emanated from his glowing cheeks.

He always wore casual attire, in fact he told me, *"No white coat, no ties-they scare my kids."*

His cards of important lab values, important papers and Viagra pen hung out of his shirt pocket.

*"I built my practice through Word of Mouth. Be nice to nurses, and spend more time with patients."* His advice was continuous, always popping out of his mouth infrequently.

He went to private practice because he doesn't want to pay $30,000 to some MBA to *"administrate me,"* he said. He rarely asked about my personal life, but I threw out some personal statements every now and then to see if he would be reeled in.

*"My parents divorced in 1992."*

*"Creighton is very focused on balance."*

*"My main motivation is to prove that 'I can,' yeah, I hear poorly, but I can do this. It isn't anger, nor greed, nor love. I experienced these feelings severely. My motivation is to empower my self-esteem."*

*"I say 'excuse me,' or 'pardon me,' almost 10,000 times a day and the embarrassment is evident."*

He was so efficient he had time to sit and listen to me every now and then. He taught me how to circumcise. Dr. Vann was the only Jewish Pediatrician offered to be the Mohel in Nebraska.

Dr. Vann's medical assistant called me the "strep man," as I could diagnose strep throat by patient history and physical examination. If I thought it was strep, I would order the strep screen and they were all positive. I still like to point out that a strep screen is not the best test. If it is positive, that means it is highly likely to be strep, but if it is negative, it doesn't rule out strep. A throat culture is the gold standard for strep throat.

# Chapter 16

## Family Practice Rotation Chronicles

*... everything on earth has a purpose, every disease an herb to cure it, and every person a mission. This is the Indian theory of existence.*

*Mourning Dove (Salish) 1888 - 1936*

The first time I got to work in the Veterans' Administration hospital in Omaha, was very exciting. Being very patriotic, it was an honor to help the vets. One man, Peter Eggside, a genteel 95 year old man told me stories about being a tank mechanic during World War 2. He told me stories such as after the war, he had to drive 44 tanks every day to help keep them up and running. The stories were both amazing and disparaging. Sometimes the vets didn't want to talk about anything. In these vets' eyes, just as Sherman said, *War is hell.*

The Band of Brothers became an HBO series, and I was an immediate and die-hard fan. Reading the book and going along with the stories, I understood what combat veterans' harrowing experiences. It made me respect them all the more.

During one of my ER shifts, I met a man who was 88 y/o, but thought he was 89, who thought his nausea was caused by constipation. He therefore took 3 milk of magnesiums, and developed diarrhea which actually worsened his volume depletion making him very dehydrated.

The problem with diarrhea is that important chemicals, such as sodium, potassium, and chloride, which are normally re-absorbed in the sigmoid colon, actually get wasted through diarrhea. This will drop the potassium levels, which if the levels get too low, can cause heart rhythm issues.

One of the problems I saw in the VA hospital was that waiting in the ER was malignant. I remember one gentleman who broke both his wrists waited on transport to the X-ray department for 2 hours. I decided to take him up in the wheelchair myself. Five hours later, we were still waiting on the Xrays. I didn't get to see him, as my shift ended. I have had visions of patients being left in the hallway waiting for their x rays to be taken. We could call them nightmares.

For the most part, people went to the ER not feeling well. Some vets have been through so much that they didn't care anymore, and we had to appeal to them to take care of themselves. Convincing them was easy, but seeing results were a different matter. When someone doesn't feel well, they are open to suggestions regarding their health, and will take whatever advice they can get. But once they feel well, they tend to forget the advice.

My presentation at the end of the VA hospital month was on *"Physical exam of a Posterior Cruciate Ligament tear."* Like other orthopod wannabes, our presentations were similar regardless of what rotation we were on. I think the only time there wasn't an orthopedic-like presentation was during OB-GYN, when I presented, *"Viral infections during Pregnancy."*

I was always a go-getter. I wasn't smart, but I had a work ethic, and strong discipline to boot. When I learn something, I take it very seriously. For instance, when I learned that Fiber reduces Cancer risks by 35-45%. It is amazing what a lecture in the Med School Hall can make you do. That same afternoon I took two fiber pills that added up to about 2 grams of fiber. I wasn't anywhere near the 20 to 30 grams recommended by the FDA. Anyway, the next day I camped out in the restroom.

I couldn't understand why people had a hard time getting up in the morning, and studying for everything early. I couldn't understand why people would waste time staying up late, going to the bar and drinking a brew. Well, except for the latter, everything else is still foreign.

It is a hard life, but I knew that I had something special. It wasn't just that I had hearing difficulties, or Native American blood, or anything less, but I had an overwhelming desire to succeed in whatever I enjoyed the most. So I researched everything that I enjoyed: triathlon training, running, cycling, writing, reading, getting published, etc... I couldn't stop printing up articles off the internet to learn more.

When I realized that I had a gift of communicating by a different medium, I set to work on writing real articles. I had enough poetry to publish 2 books. Personally, I think anyone can do poetry, and poems are basically songs without music. I had knowledge about nursing and medicine. Having worked in both fields gave me a clear advantage in the clinical world. I could bring all these components together to write something and anything medical.

I knew how to treat the nurses, how to run "codes," how to act professionally. I knew I could share it, so I did. I wrote for the Creighton University Wellness Chronicle.

At first, my articles were just a waste of paper, because I tried too hard to be funny. I slowly learned how to be sarcastic which a lot of medical students became. There was something to be said about all the knowledge, and how far we could go with sarcasm. Any of my medical school colleagues could attest to my ridiculous overtures during the talent shows we put on. When I decided I wasn't gaining ground I began writing "how to" articles, mostly for the medical students.

I thought about promoting myself, but stopped short of trying. Realizing it would be hard to get ahead in any career if you can't comfortably claim your achievements, I started planning. I felt it might be ok to be deaf and still have something to give back to the public.

My inferiority complex felt like a monkey on my back, but I continued to strive for acceptance. I thought hard about what I could do. Randall told me to toot my horn anytime I had a chance. I always thought that was hanky panky. But I remember him too well, and I wanted to be like him.

So I decided to write down my 5 greatest strengths to read them aloud everyday until I could comfortably promote myself in any networking situation. This began as a hobby and quickly became an exercise in futility. The statements took quite a bit of time to come up with. But here goes:

*"I am a dedicated professional with clinical experience totaling up to 10 years of direct patient contact."*
*"I am a team player who communicates with all departments-lab, xray, physicians, nurses, and administration in order to give the best management of care."*

*"My discipline is 2nd to none as I have demonstrated throughout my career."*

*"I have run marathons, and completed an Ironman Triathlon after Step I of the boards."*

*"I have written an Ebook, published a freelancing article, and continued to pursue my desire to finish my autobiography on med school success with a hearing impairment."*

Of course, I didn't read these aloud everyday, but just coming up with the statements made me feel normal, like I could give something back to society. I began writing articles and trying to get published. One of my articles got published in a journal on Family in Colorado. I was so thrilled when I received a check for my writing.

# Chapter 17

## Mocha, Mondays, and Retarded Mentals

*What you say?*

*Are you wearing hearing aids?*
*I'm sorry what did you say?*
*Are you wearing hearing aids?*
*Oh yes, that is they.*
*How did you lose your hearing?*
*I never had it to begin with.*
*I can't believe that is what you're wearing.*
*I'm sorry for my thick lisp.*
*Oh no don't worry about that at all!*
*I too like the leaves in the Fall!*
*Hee hee haw haw haw!*
*What is up with yall?*
*Did you just hear what I said?*
*Is that why your face is red?*

*Justus Peters MD*

It is now my last year of medical school in the Fall 2004, and I had some mental numbness and started thinking philosophically. This chapter should probably be called, *"The More You Know, the Less You Know."*

One of the issues that arise in every medical student's life is the realities of endless knowledge. The sky itself would not be a barrier to the endless volumes. After 2 years of basic sciences, I was tired of reading and rereading everything. I wanted to know. I needed to know the extent to my knowledge. Is it sufficient for passing or is it sufficient for giving advice?

More ominous-but much more rare-possibility is that we can get over-confidant with the knowledge. Thereby, we'd give advice to others prematurely without being certified.

So I developed a way to constantly give myself feedback for the learning that took place the past two years. I solely answered written questions. One, I can read, and two, I don't have to hear the question. Many an opinion was made of possible mental retardation after I would answer a question inappropriately. But this written question strategy was a no-brainer.

Question answering compounds a routine-a style, a circulation-almost habit forming study technique. Answering with correct logical sense increased my test taking skills. I developed a habit of perpetuating the vast complexities of facts into my memory bank.

Sometimes it was not so subtle-like when I answered wrong (I counted) 9 times in small group for Heme-Onc rotation in the course of 2 hours. People began talking about how stupid I must have been. When in fact, I was molding what I thought I knew into something that was concrete.

Geniuses ask questions to answer all the time. Now I am no genius, but I know that geniuses were answering a lot of questions, and I was answering a lot of questions too.

Sometimes it was simple absentmindedness when I mistook the Hepatic Artery for the Inferior Vena Cava-a large mistake especially since I was giving a presentation on Surgical Disease of the Liver during my Surgery Rotation to the Chairman of the department!

Other times, I was more subtle, going through a question book from Kaplan, NMS, or other text in the social confines of Borders or Barnes & Noble bookstores. A wrong answer helped me learn without the social embarrassment in the classroom.

I needed feedback, and it came in the form of wrong answered questions. Where was my logic? Why did I miss that? Well of course, it was the minutiae of information that I didn't care about during lectures at one point. Or it could have been that I knew it but forgot it in the depths of grey matter.

Regardless, I was able to find what I did and didn't know. It was humbling, and at times uplifting. It created my self esteem in medicine, and stripped it away. I was constantly learning everyday.

Reading questions with a friend is even better, because now you have a 2 way street in the learning process. Reading with more people would be fine, but you lose the spotlight easily because there is bound to be more than a couple people who already know the answer.

Every Monday morning I went to the drive through at Crane Coffee, or Scooters Java Express for my weekly shot of Mocha freeze with extra expresso. The mornings were somber. Skies were gray, sometimes dark. The sun rarely rose up early. The radio cackled with Todd and Tyler in the morning 92.3 FM. Oh, yes, may the expresso open my eyes.

I never drank coffee until after college, and by this time I felt related to Kaldi and his dancing goats, as I consumed coffee like a coffee pot. Kaldi, legend has it, was the shepherd who wondered why his goats were dancing and noticed them eating a red fruit, so he started consuming them, and the rest is history.

Coffee was a good philosophy inducer. I wondered about medicine in more than just the art form. I wondered about the social impact, business, and management of care.

How do we, as public servants, healers of the sick, end up not desiring to, but forced to scramble for knowledge about business, in turn destroying the very fabric that is essential to healing? Because of the loopholes, and laws of business, physicians need more knowledge than ever about the idiosyncrasies of business to manage a successful practice. Dallas-based Physicians Resource Group Inc. filed for protection under Chapter 11 Bankruptcy, along with many other Texan clinics. The need to learn about the medical management side of medicine has pressured many physicians from the ability to just enjoy taking care of people.

*"Our skills are way up here, and an accountant's skills are down here."* Dr. Stephen Gruba, a rural Family Practice Physician in Iowa stated with his hand up above his head for physician's skills, and way low by his waist when talking about accountants' skills. *"We need to discern these facts to build better practices,"* He concluded.

What derails us in our quest to instill health, through research, hours and hours of labor and toil on the wards, and sleepless nights on-call. What has caused such disillusionment? Such disenchantment as I have ever known in my life exists within the ranks of medicine because what little moderation in costs of the healthcare crisis existed is kaput, and costs are rising.

Managed Care. The very word, "Care," should be substituted with the term, "illness." Because "care" is something we do that is not manageable, but innate as it comes from our hearts, our desires that beset us from the tiny toddler days with dreams of being a doctor and carrying our little black bag and stethoscope. "Care," is enabling the patient to become healthy if not healthier than its present state. How is shortcutting through diagnostic tests, and practicing defensive medicine helping? How many doctors think to themselves the cases that poured through their offices that could have been if only I could do this test, or that, I could better manage my patient's illness. The American Medical Student Association website reports that around 71% of physicians believe they can do a better job without worrying about costs of care.

If corporate management is reducing costs, which it is not, why is the price we pay the compassion and care, the trusted fiduciary agreement between physician and patient, that social service for the betterment of humankind? Is Managed Illness actually caring? Are the cost cutting loopholes, headaches, and practice of defensive medicine prolonging illness?

What help is the legal symposium doing for medicine? Driving up malpractice insurance rates, sending doctors on strikes, and other states to practice where there is tort reform. In Mississippi Jefferson county, almost 200 million dollars have been awarded to two parties. The trial lawyers talk about how "they" (meaning the tort reform advocates like ourselves) want to keep hurting the poor people, keep the ill people unwell, etc. In fact, the millions of uninsured Americans can't afford healthcare because of the trial lawyers' inadequacy to restrain their greedy money mongrel selves from suing which drives all prices up anyway.

Case in point, one malpractice lawyer, senator is John Edwards (D-NC) who made his fortune by suing physicians. He parades as a hero protecting patients' rights when efforts do squat for managed care and the uninsured poor. Fox News' Radley Balko reported in his article that John Edwards co-sponsored a bill on patient's rights version that would have permitted trial lawyers to bypass any state tort reform law and to sue healthcare providers for punitive damages in federal court. The Employment Policy Foundation estimated at the time the Edwards Bill would result in 56,000 more lawsuits per year and a $16 billion increase in healthcare costs. Now how are our uninsured helpless poor doing because of this? Why John Edwards says he is helping the helpless is beyond me. Note: this was my opinion back in 2004, which is prior to his vice-president campaign and efforts for possible presidential candidacy. So I was not in any way swayed by public opinion after his affair on his wife while she was suffering from breast cancer.

As a young, albeit older medical student, aspiring doctor to be, it breaks my heart to see the audacious cycle perpetuate itself and can only hope that my endeavor to be an advocate for all medical professionals in the journey to serve the public, will restore precious hope and trust in our patients, our families, and ourselves.

Okay, back to earth, and back to the simple task of medicine. I'm not going to fix anything complaining about it. I'll just go out and do the best I can.

# Chapter 18

## Psych Rotation

*Anxiety, Depression and Bipolar*

*I can't go outside, my heart will pound,*
*I hate looking at myself, my face too round,*
*Why can't I sleep at night,*
*I have no interest to write.*
*What guilt haunts my soul, and sucks my energy.*
*Concentrate? Can't, appetite? None,*
*Who cares when, where, what I'll be?*
*Into a bottomless pit, all hope is gone.*
*Why do you look at me like that?*
*I'll smash your face so flat!*
*I'm the King of the World!*
*Not getting out of bed today,*
*There is just no way jose.*
*What's hidden you can plainly see,*
*But what is one more plastic surgery?*

*A look into mental illness*
*Justus Peters MD*
*2/24/2012*

On my first psychological case with Munchausen by Proxy I learned a lot about the realities of the world. Is it reality that this much craziness exists? Munchausen is when someone invents or exaggerates medical symptoms, sometimes engaging in self-harm, to gain attention or sympathy. So Munchausen by proxy is when the care-giver does so. Since 1994, Psychiatry renamed it to "factitious disorder by proxy." They may inflict injury or sickness upon themselves so that their caregiver/parent will not leave them.

The more I read about this syndrome the more aghast I would become that people would do this to themselves or to their children. Some of the cautions include:

A highly attentive parent who is reluctant to leave their child's side and who themselves seem to require constant attention.

A child who has one or more medical problems that do not respond to treatment or that follow an unusual course that is persistent, puzzling and unexplained.

Physical or laboratory findings that are highly unusual, discrepant with history, or physically or clinically impossible.

A parent who appears to be unusually calm in the face of serious difficulties in their child's medical course while being highly supportive and encouraging of the physician or who is angry, devalues staff, and demands further intervention, more procedures, second opinions, and transfers to other, more sophisticated facilities.

In 90% of cases, the mother is the abuser. The important thing to know is that this syndrome is a behavior not a psychological diagnosis. I also learned that as a physician, this behavior shouldn't surprise me.

It would be easy to say that I was naïve still, but the fact was that I have never experienced anything in psychiatry. The more I learned, the more I realized that a lot of Psychiatry is real, and the science behind it is repeatable and good science. What the case taught me was that people inherently are not evil but can be evil not just to other people but themselves. Then again, we are taught that perception of life is individual, and what I think is evil, may be in fact normal behavior in someone else's view.

The rotation gave me a lot of insight on ethical dilemmas.

I remember watching a German film in med school Ethics Class, „I Accuse! (Ich klage an!)." In this movie, a woman with multiple sclerosis asks her husband, a doctor, to permanently relieve her of her suffering. He agrees to give her a lethal injection of morphine. At his trial he argues that he committed an act of mercy, not murder. He is acquitted.

Personally, I felt like he murdered his wife. If doing no harm is an oath, didn't this man perform the worst act of being a doctor? According to ethics, it depends. The legal world has penetrated medicine to its core, and therefore, it could be legal to do harm to a patient. But in my own personal opinion regarding medical ethics, philosophy trumps the law, and I will not ever perform physician-assisted suicide.

In the hospice setting, when we treat pain and suffering, we use high doses of morphine, or anxiety medications. This is not physician assisted suicide as we are relieving the suffering as one is actively dying.

An interesting lesson regarding the Placebo affect is recorded in my diary. In the lectures, we had Alternative healers discuss how their science works. Natural healing is independent of treatment protocol. A response to any treatment protocol includes physiological response as well as emotional.

Because the responses cause changes in lifestyle, it can vary by culture or by disease. With this premise, they say Alternative medicine works as well or better than conventional medicine by maximizing the response.

We were advised that we could also maximize western medicine efficacy by adapting some practical aspects of alternative care. They reported that no matter what, we would always have patients who practiced alternative therapies and we would have to deal with them and understand them.

I understand very well the amount of holistic and alternative therapies out there, and respect their theories. If it works it works. Everyone is different and can respond

Opposite of the Placebo affect is the Nocebo affect which increases chances of adverse reactions. This effect occurs when the belief of the patient is toward a negative reaction instead of a positive reaction. For instance, when we prescribe Prozac for depression, because it takes up to 3 weeks to start working, patients may develop a nocebo effect where they experience adverse effects such as headaches and sleep disturbances.

The Psychiatry rotation instilled a respect for the brain. The brain can make patients see things, hear things, and smell things that are not there. The brain can make a schizophrenic live in a wonderland and never want to return to reality, as easy as it allows a normal person exist in reality.

I remember the patient actors and actresses who "play-acted" their disease process and we were graded on how well we listened, how our diction sounded, and how much compassion we showed. It was good practice, and I just now remember that it was part of the Art of Medicine. Included in the Art are all the other modalities

— chiropractic, naturopathic, osteopathic and Eastern Medicines.

# Chapter 19

## Bones and Groans

*To be an Orthopedic Surgeon*

*The nights I toil and slave,*
*To learn, to fix, to be*
*A surgeon once I craved,*
*To learn the anatomy,*
*And heal a broken bone,*
*Or heal the suffered lame,*
*To hear no more groan.*
*But like all times before,*
*I go not where I know,*
*I've failed again once more,*
*To ground I fall below.*

*Justus Peters MD*
*2/14/12*

I always wanted to be an Orthopedic surgeon. Every since I circulated in the OR and watched the guys hammering and sawing away, I knew this was what I wanted to do. Dr. Murphy could finish a knee joint replacement in such little time, he spent most of his time suturing everything back together. I was amazed at how much these guys enjoyed their job.

My first experience with orthopedics which literally means "straight child," included a case where a baby was born with a congenital dislocation of her hip. The case I watched was fascinating with the Orthopedic Surgeon doing "abduction splinting." It never would be easy to put a splint or cast on a child running around. I thought it ironic that modern medicine used general anesthesia for casting. It worked.

Since then surgical treatments include core decompressions or total hip replacements. All I could do was hand him some crutches to take some of the weight-bearing load off his hips. I learned that Blount disease was the most common problem after 3 years of age. Bowlegged people always looked weird, and I never knew why until this rotation.

When the inside of the knee joint matures before the rest of the knee, the angulation occurs. In medical jargon, the medial proximal tibia ossifies abnormally. Again, the treatment depends on the age. The young children get conservative treatment, while the older child undergoes aggressive treatment. Before age 5, bracing is used, and after that is surgical.

I met Dr. McGuire, the orthopedic surgeon at Creighton University who was quite possibly the most important man I would ever meet. He would become my advisor, and help me get to my career goals. I actually remember my first encounter with him. It was like yesterday.

*"Hi, I'm Justus Peters."* I said slightly nervous. Of course I was nervous — he could make or break my career.

*"And you need what?"* he asked. As if everyone needs something from him. Wow, that kind of sucks. The sad part was I didn't really get to know him or get him to know me. He just went straight to the problem.

*"I need to show you some papers."* I said.

*"Oh for faculty advisor?"* he asked. How did he know?!?

*"Yes."* I replied, smiling surprised.

He continued, *"and you need a letter of recommendation?"*

Okay, I was creeped out. He knew exactly what I wanted, which didn't bode well for me. *"All the above,"* I said. Obviously this man isn't go-

ing to give me the time of day to get to know me.
I was a bug that he probably wanted to step on.

Sure enough, a little while later, he asked
me, *"what's your name again?"* I really couldn't blame
him. In my class, there were about 10 of us who
wanted to be orthopedic surgeons.

One case I won't ever forget was a 5 y/o boy
came in with the mother complaining of a fever
followed by pain in his knee. I thought it could
be an infection, like maybe just a septic joint.
That would have been easy, just a hip aspiration
of joint contents, send it to the lab and await the
results. But the resident ordered a bone scan.

*"Why the bone scan?"* I asked, trying not to act
too surprised lest I be considered ill-knowledged.

*"Have to rule out osteomyelitis."* He said without
missing a beat.

Osteomyelitis is an infection of the bone
and its surrounding tissues. This isn't good. Antibiotics for 6 weeks can change the gut flora completely. The problem is a "bug-less" gut doesn't
work. We need those bugs to break down our stool
for nutrients.

It was during my Children's hospital ortho rotation that I learned I couldn't really fix
children. They fixed themselves. We cut them,
opened them up, put metal into the bodies, and
discharged them to rehab centers to get better on
their own. The childrens' immune systems were

working overtime to heal, and they healed very fast.

We gave joint injections all the time. Synvisc and corticosteroid injections had equal efficacy, so we planned our joint replacements after a certain amount of time with injection protocols.

It was hard to look at the human body as an automobile. The compassion I had was replaced by this robotic procedure mentality. Let's fix 'em and street 'em was the rally cry it seemed.

This was in direct confrontation with my personality. I wasn't a robot, and I had compassion for my patients. I cared when people felt pain, suffering, and illness. I still felt like ortho was what I wanted to do. It was going to be hard work though.

I knew I had to shine and rise to the occasion. I learned how to repair lacerations by suturing one handed. Nope not good enough. I went to the casting class, and wow, not even close. I felt like Monty Python's actors trying to put a cast on. It was sadly funny.

Our school was next to the Boys Town National Research hospital, so we spent many mornings reviewing and caring for children with unusual presentations.

I learned how to do abduction splinting of a congenital dislocation of the hip. It is much easier done under anesthesia.

One day in clinic we had a 6 year old boy with decreased hip motion and occasional knee pain. He ambulated by protecting his painful side, which is what we call "antalgic gait." On X ray he had "avascular necrosis." Avascular necrosis is defined as cellular death of bone components due to interruption of the blood supply; the bone structures then collapse, resulting in bone destruction, pain, and loss of joint function.

While there was no uniform treatment standards, the management depended on how bad the joint destruction was. The worse the destruction, the more likely surgery was needed.

The orthopods rarely had an emergency surgery to do unless an open fracture occurred. An open fracture is when a piece of fractured bone is visible through lacerated skin.

Other ortho emergencies I encountered were infected joints, which required surgery to "clean out the joint," aka "open arthrotomy."

We had a gentleman who had chronic osteomyelitis, who was continuously on antibiotics and required multiple surgeries to clean out the infected bone. Usually we can tell is someone is getting osteomyelitis by a history of febrile illness followed by bone pain. Then we ordered the bone scan.

I thought I wanted to be an orthopedic surgeon, until I learned my USMLE step 1 score. It wasn't high enough, which essentially discouraged me from attempting to get in. I was going to try my best when I had my outside rotations though. I picked Galveston and San Antonio orthopedics rotations in the Spring of my 4th year.

*Diary entry: 2/4/2004*

*I'm told over and over again work hard and I do, I get the cold shoulder.*

*I'm told over and over again to take initiative – I do by writing progress notes and I get the cold shoulder. I'm told to teach the M3's so I do, and what do I get? I'm confused, bedraggled, and pissed off because you guys know that I want to do orthopedics, and if I am doing something wrong, and unable to mesh, then we have a serious issue.*

*I feel like Jerry Maguire, you know, when he has been rejected by every one of his players and he is working his ass off to sell himself to someone, anyone, and he ends up screaming, "Show me the money!!!!!" and keeps one of his players. The only real thing I got going for me is my discipline, motivation, and ambition to succeed. I ask each of you what I can do more and I'm pissed because no one tells me anything.*

*I'm starting to get mighty disappointed in this month's rotation b/c I heard UNMC is a whole lot bet-*

*ter, and I didn't realize that Dr. Maguire lets us write our own recommendation letters. So naturally, I'm pissed. I'm pissed b/c I make a mistake and you guys bash me like I'm an idiot. I'm pissed b/c there is little teaching, a whole lot of gossip and patient bashing going on here. I know you guys are not happy here, but don't take it out on me. I need your help. I can't do it without you. I want to help you. I need you to help me help you. Like in fracture conference, I didn't understand what the heck that bony tumor thing was on a patient's hip Xray.*

Writing it down and asking the chief about it later helped me learn what "Heterotopic Ossification," was. I was told to read about it. I did. Next day, I was pimped on it, and I got pimped so bad, it looked ugly.

*"What did you find out about HO?"* The chief asked. Pimping is not literal, it means asking questions. The person asking the questions "pimp" another person. It is slang, and the first time I heard it I was 2nd year medical student. Pimping can literally feel like getting raped — albeit mentally, which is how I felt this particular time.

It was my chance to shine. I perked up somewhat and answered, *"It is an extra-tissue growth of bone."* The questions didn't get any better.

I understood that the basic tenet of pimping was to figure out what you don't know by answering questions. This also opened up a major issue with me. How did I learn all these years? No one asked me questions like this before. I found out an easier way to learn, but I was 20 years behind the times. All those years, I took my books home and read them to learn myself. No one spent extra time with me asking questions verbally.

The questions continued, *"Why does it happen?"*

*"What is the prevalence and incidence of HO?"*

*"How do you manage it?"*

It was obvious I didn't study hard enough, as question after question was asked. Feeling demoralized from my orthopedic rotation experience, I realized it was not cut out for me. But the extra work I put into it by staying all night up with the residents and orthopedic surgeries may have been just a self-esteem boost for me. That was my half-full optimistic assumption.

I wondered back on one of the topics on osteoporosis we learned. Osteoporosis is when the bone weakens. The bone cells that break down bone, and the cells that build bone are not in sync, so there is bone loss. I learned that increased stress raises cortisol levels. Increased cortisol sucks out bone matrix, causing osteoporosis. I had a distant urge to get a bone scan for myself.

After Orthopedics I was burned out. The next month's rotation — Diagnostic Radiology — was basically showing up every other morning for noon conference. Only one of the residents cared about teaching us. The rest of the month, you could sit around and act like you were listening. I made a small presentation on CXR (chest x-ray) signs for the medical student. I looked up all the signs on the Internet and made a Powerpoint presentation for the teaching resident. He seemed impressed. At least I accomplished something.

# Chapter 20
## Death and Despair

*Heart Attack*

*It comes and goes, waxes and wanes so dull,*
*Aching, throbbing pain right here in my chest,*
*My neck and arm burns with such cramp-like pulls,*
*Spouse thinks the emergency room is best,*
*I pop a second nitro under tongue,*
*The pain is not so bad now I believe.*
*My feet and legs floating away so numb,*
*The pressure now upon my chest relieved,*
*Spouse watching me with those green teary eyes,*
*Those green seas I have loved for many years,*
*I need to tell my kids my last goodbyes.*
*Unable to move 'tis the end I fear,*
*My wife my love her wet lips kissing mine,*
*This restful sleep is peace and then goodbye.*

*8/8/10*
*Justus Peters MD*

The patient's ventilator hummed and oxygenated life into the dying man. He is old and gray; sickness smells of rubbing alcohol on sweat soaked skin. His intravenous hep-lock exists only for high doses of Versed and Morphine. His bilateral chest tubes — inserted just a few minutes before — allow better ventilation the only salvation for pleural effusions.

His family sits somber around his bed. Downcast eyes glance upon the monitor. Back to the patient, and back to the monitor. Hope and despair in a sad ballet dance. Hands holding hands, some tight, some loose. A tear drops, a tissue used, and a sniffle heard. The tired heart beeps intermittently, marching with the ventilator's hum.

My eyes take on the scene in an eerily glaze. I have not seen this moment in medicine ever before. Medical school has not taught me much about the hardness — yet tenderness of death. We had the "Dying with Dignity" test after watching a video on hospice care. We had the mock interviews with actors & actresses giving them bad news. Someone lost a baby. Someone lost a loved one. We argued in Ethics class about benevolence, the Hippocratic Oath, and assisted suicide. But I have not ever managed the care of a dying person.

My thoughts churned and visualizing a younger man emerged. A dashing lively humorist walks with his wife. Limber joints, a racing heart, and romance smiling at his love. With this I began to emphasize. Will I be in this bed with a wife too? Will I be surrounded by family? What will I have if I am alone in death as I have been alone in the silence of life?

This old tired man lived through experience — real life, emotions, and illness. He had pride, humility, love, jealousy, triumph, and depression. He probably farmed the land, earned his high school diploma, and worked at a grocery store. He probably joined the army and fought in Normandy. He may have been in the Pacific theatre. He may have run the beaches of Iwo Jima, he may have held grandbabies, and laughed about jokes. He may have yelled and lost his temper. He may have held and kissed his wife a million times. He probably did it all.

I became saddened with the family, but held firm. I asked the family if they wanted to pray. They looked at each other and thought about it. The daughter went to the wife and they whispered to each other. The daughter came to me and said it would be very nice.

I don't pray with patients, and I realize the integrity of different religions. Some people are spiritual and some are not. But I know when a patient is in need. I know when the family needs strength. Particularly at the door of death, do families become more religious or spiritual. They wonder at the closeness of what lies beyond. What happens when the last breath is taken?

They wonder at how fragile life is finally. However, I was nervous and my adrenaline flowed as I began a prayer. It was a simple one.

Afterwards, when the mortician left with the body, the family came to me. They gave me what I gave them, reassurance and hope. I knew then what the key to compassion is. It is the same that enables us to help others in time of need. It is the same that conquers our pride and makes us pay the Salvation Army bell-ringers. To open doors for others, to smile at the grocery check out lane.  It is the same that reminds us of our weaknesses and our strength. It reminds us to be humble. It is empathy.

Each soul is perfect in each human being. Some souls are rugged from brutal experiences, some naïve from innocence. Yet the soul of my fellow man and woman are perfect — as perfect as I have been molded from the Creator. It is with this idea of salvation for all, that I steady my heart in understanding another human with empathy.

Understanding the soul of one with problems — both mental and physical — enables one to be objective and empathetic. We encounter all sorts of patients, in all sorts of needs and despairs. Each is unique regardless of circumstance. Greedy needs test our emotional strength. Trauma tests our physical strength. Medicine tests our devotion to the soul. Yet when we realize beyond their stone cold hearts, their impassable walls, a perfect little soul remains, then we can continue our journey into the healing of another.

I certainly felt I had to lean on the Creator when I received my 3rd rejection from the Indian Health Service (IHS). Creighton University was an expensive endeavor, and I will probably be paying on this school loan for the rest of my life, so thinking ahead, I desperately wanted to be with the military or the IHS.

Donnette was with me when I learned that I was rejected by the IHS the 3rd time. Surprising myself with a wail that seemed inhuman with despair, I felt crushed.

During med school, I couldn't catch a break. I tried first to get into the Navy, but my hearing was too bad, so I failed. Then I tried to get into the Air Force, which failed. I tried the army and failed. My hearing kept me from doing what I wanted to do which was treat our soldiers, or treat my people, and serve my country.

Like most all Native Americans, pride in America, is paramount. We love the land and Mother Earth, and this is our home. Our home is also the United States of America, and I wanted to do whatever it takes to sacrifice for it. I was willing to be a soldier to the depths of my soul. To me, honor and integrity are ingrained through tradition. To not be able to serve the U.S. was a failure in my eyes. And again, I was so angry at not being able to hear normally.

In instances where I failed, or learned by some tragic accident, I cursed the day I was diagnosed as deaf. But in successes, my curse would "become" only a small barrier. So it would be a matter of time before I would feel good about myself after this rejection.

When one of my the patients that I became close to lost 15 lbs. in 3 weeks, and was yellow for a week, the family all came in to support him during his hospital stay.

My 65 year old male patient had the signs and symptoms of the one disease that the medical community continues to battle. Painless jaundice and weight loss spells disaster. I have rarely seen a patient go home alive, but Tom did. He was my patient and I enjoyed taking care of him.

*The name of this patient has been changed to protect his privacy

When he asked questions about why he was yellow, I wrote on his dry-erase board the anatomy of the liver and gallbladder and explained how bilirubin gets broken down. His family all sat around me with their eyes glued to my art. Although I am no artist, their attention encouraged me. I felt like I was painting a story for them, and their attention was a respectful gratification.

His son asked questions about the problem with his gallbladder. I explained that the Porcelain Gallbladder found on CT scan has a 20% chance of being Cholangiocarcinoma. I began to research information for them. They kept asking questions, and I kept answering based on the research the night before.

*"Cholangiocarcinoma risks are increased with gallstones, ulcerative colitis, pancreatic reflux, sclerosing cholangitis...."* I would continue and they would listen. Fifteen or so individuals packed in the room created an atmosphere of support, love, and the desire to learn about their ill family member.

I continued, *"40% of Cholangiocarcinoma can be partially resected, and even when that occurs, the patient has a 10% chance of survival from dying of cholangitis."*

The numbers confused them, so I wrote down numbers.

*"For every 100 people who come in with the same kind of yellow and weight loss, with this CT finding, only 40 of them can have a 1 in 10 chance of surviving the entire ordeal."* That made sense to them.

I would see Tom early in the morning, and later in the evening before going home. He would get a Cholecystectomy, a Duodenal repair, and a Gastrojejunostomy, and a biliary stent placed in his bile duct. His hospital course ran 10 days, and I enjoyed his company, and he remembered my name every visit.

174 A WALK IN MY MOCCASINS

*"Hey Justus! How is my man? Have you met my brother?"* He would say.

*"Hey Justus! How's my doctor? Have you met my daughter and grandbaby?"*

I looked forward to the greetings each morning. Someone, a family member, would always be in the room with him. The power of family was instilled in me. It increased my respect for treatment encompassing not only the patient but the family as well. Advising, listening, and encouraging the family members became a daily plan for me.

Now Tom is at home with home health care. For a while I was receiving updates via telephone on how he was doing. He doesn't have long to live, but his family is there for him, and that is what really matters.

Now as a 4th year medical student, I had the opportunity to be working at the hospital when he came in for the last time. His daughter emailed me and told me where he was at. I visited him, but he was sent to Interventional Radiology to get a stent placed. This stent was to enable him to release bile into his small intestine. When it builds up it can cause complications like infections and jaundice.

He remembered me when I leaned over to encourage him lying on the cold operation table. His eyes held a flicker of recognizance. His cold hand, whittled from his losing battle to cancer, seemed small in my hands. My warmth enveloped his coldness. A small tear streamed down the side of his face.

The next day I came by to see how he was doing. He was terminal. His family surrounded him.

*"Is there anything I can do?"* I asked the daughter.

*"No, it is great that you can be here."* She replied.

I put my hand on her shoulder. She came into my arms. Tom's wife gave me a hug. The two sons shook my hand and thanked me for helping out so much.

I told the surgery department secretary to page me when his pulse decreased. My plan was to rush up there to be with the family in the last moments. I didn't make it.

My heart beats for my patients. Their families — part of the cure, must be encouraged and taught as the patient is treated. For this experience to enrich me I had to lose a favorite patient of mine.

Consequently, I make the effort to treat everyone fairly.

The last December in medical school, I went on a Caribbean cruise for the first time. As a fourth year medical student I was finishing out a major chapter in life. The cruise became a metaphor. I traversed unknown waters, witnessed some amazing stories, hit some rough spots and some storms. Experiencing it the best way I knew how and surviving was another cornerstone.

Getting to this point and embarking on a new journey was exciting. I did it for myself, maybe to prove something, but maybe not. What those close to me think of me is becoming less and less of a burden. I don't carry depression or anxiety on my shoulders regarding my deafness. Knowing that I have done what few have done before became a sense of pride.

The Spring of my last year in medical school was surreal. I had a few interviews to make and my orthopedic dreams were dashed as I had only one interview at University of Texas Medical School Branch (UTMB.) I didn't have one at University of Texas San Antonio (UTSA) where I spent a month working as hard as I could possibly muster to make it. Even though my dream was orthopedics, I tried to the very last possible moment. I did get a Transitional year internship at El Paso, and although I didn't get what I dreamed of getting, I was happy to have a job.

When I had time to think, I decided to join the Freemasons and become a Shriner. I felt like the wrinkles have been wrung out of me, and that I could improve myself in philosophical

ways. My Uncle Red, whose real name was Pat
Turney was a Grandmaster, and he told me about
the Masons. He said they will make a good man
better. So I was happy to join the brotherhood and
feel like I belonged to a group.

I felt like I came full circle now that I
was graduating, and that the connection with
the Shriners was for developing and nurturing
friendships. I was in the motor patrol and drove a
motorcycle in drills and parades for El Maida of El
Paso, and later for El Moslah of Fort Worth.

My mother and sister Becky came down for
the graduation was shared with my mother one
of my sisters, and my new-in-laws. Donnette and
I got married 2 weeks prior. We honeymooned in
Jamaica, where we laid on the beach enjoying the
surf and sand. We snorkeled among the reefs.

Doing things I never thought possible
brightened my view of life. Life itself was meant
to be lived on the outside, not on the inside where
I have spent my first 30 years.

# Chapter 21

## The Trail of Two Turtles

*Internship*

*The practice of medicine thus begins,*
*The test of wisdom and truth within,*
*My mind, my heart, my soul with hope.*
*Around my neck hangs a stethoscope,*
*A new pristine dry cleaned white coat*
*A fresh white pad to write my note,*
*A badge of honor my name with MD,*
*The knowledge to fight death and disease,*
*My tuning fork for hearing, my tape measure,*
*Black and blue pen, bandage scissors,*
*Internship survival guide, medicine for dummies,*
*A deck of cards for call night rummy.*
*A pager and phone ready for calls,*
*Ready to heal one and all.*

*Justus Peters MD*

The first time I had a long white coat with my name on it was certainly one of my proudest moments. Many thoughts ran through my head. Am I good enough to take care of people? Am I competent? Will I miss that cardiac murmur? Do I finally get a little respect?

As silly as some thoughts were, most were serious. The white coat was used for protection against blood, bodily fluids, waste, and other mucosi of species unbeknownst. It was also a signal to my brain that I serve the public when I wear it. Although I felt pride when I wore it, I knew that being humble was far better. I donated my life to public service. After all, it was this wonderful American Republic that gave me the opportunity to serve as a physician.

Both the resilience and the fragility of the human body impress me to provide a most generalized healthy management program for my patients. Experiencing both the beginning and the end of life, and all that is between, I am charged with the duty to preserve life, and respect death. The employment of Medicine within our public system should strive for health in all areas of life. The white coat I put on seemed at times a heavy burden to bear. And in my Intern year, the first year out of medical school, I felt that burden many times.

Internship in the Transitional program at El Paso Texas Tech Health Science Center was an adequate beginning. The hospital was literally a few blocks from the Mexico Border. It is a modern looking albeit small hospital with 6 floors. It is designated to treat the President and other US Administrators if they travel in the region. One of the fondest memories I have include carrying a Venti Mocha Frappucino from Starbucks up to the hospital every morning. The Latina cooks made the best breakfast chorizo burritos.

Many emergency room nights gave me some unbelievable experiences. For posterity, I will share a few. One morning in the ER, a man and his wife were trying to get a trailer hitched onto a truck. An accident of some sort occurred where the truck suddenly ran over the spouse. She was brought in with a large laceration on her anterior front lower right leg that was oozing blood. She also had on X-ray a compound comminuted tibia fracture in 3 places. She needed acute orthopedic surgery right away. It later turned out that the man's truck was an automatic, and he was charged with DUI. Although an accident, they still happen.

The first few days after Christmas, we received several young teenagers into the ER who weren't wearing helmets during their excited treks on their new 4-wheelers. This was truly a holiday killer.

I delivered my first babies in this hospital, and am very grateful to the many young Mexican girls who crossed over the border in order to give their children a better life. It is hard to believe but the best training for our OB-Gyns were the baby making machines of the Mexicans.

The first time I ever pronounced a patient dead was in my intern year. When I heard the nurse I had to ask again, *"excuse me?"*

*"We need you to pronounce the patient."* She answered.

She told me where the patient was and hung up the phone. I set the phone back in the cradle. It was the first time reality hit me regarding pronouncing. I have seen death occur before in the ICU and the ER. I have seen it and it didn't surprise me. However, I have never pronounced a patient dead before. I've seen the doctors on television pronounce a patient. In action war movies, the infantryman or medic would check carotid arteries and then shake their heads. But no one taught me "the process." There is a process?

The way a lot of doctors learn is by being thrust into these situations. I obviously was expected to know this stuff, therefore, I better learn it quick. I thought it was weak to call my upper level resident to help me. In ideal situations, the upper level resident teaches the intern everything. But after a long day of rounds and lectures, they just want to go home.

I consulted my internship guide, and read all the physical assessments to do. It was 0200 hours and my adrenaline felt like fire through my veins. My heavy tired eyes instantly wide awake. I was amazed at how far I have come — from watching from the sidelines, to working the cardiac arrests, now to pronouncing someone dead. The responsibility was numbing and de-escalated my adrenaline rush.

I read to find out about the circumstances of the death. Well, the nurse told me so it must be true I thought to myself. But was the patient a do not resuscitate? Or a full code? Was it expected or sudden? Are their any family members present? All these questions I should have asked the nurse, but she assumed I already knew or would eventually find out.

I continued to read,

*"Confirm the details on the circumstances of death with the caregivers. Review the chart for important medical (length of illness, cause of death) and family issues. (Who is family? What faith? Is there a clergy contact?)"*

Well this was going to take longer than I thought. I suddenly realized "what if I am called for an emergency right now while I am trying to pronounce this patient?" That would be a dilemma I didn't want to find myself in. I quickly read over the rest of the information.

It continued:

*"Find out if an autopsy has ever been requested, or subject of organ donation been broached? In the room, ask*

*the nurse or chaplain to accompany you. Introduce yourself
to family if they are present. Ask each person their name
and relationship to the patient and shake hands with each.
Say something empathic: 'I'm sorry for your loss.'"*

I paused. Do I tell them this before or after
I pronounce the patient? I continued to read:

*"Explain what you are doing, and tell family they
can stay if they wish while you examine their loved one.
Ask what questions the family has. If you cannot answer,
contact someone who can."*

Then I read about actually pronouncing
the patient, all of these assessments were taught
in medical school, so I knew basically what to do.
It read,

*"Identify the patient, note the general appearance
of the body, test for verbal or tactile stimuli. Overtly painful stimuli are not required. Nipple or testicle twisting, or
deep sternal pressure, are inappropriate and unnecessary."*
I paused and thought, *"Really? Do you think
anyone would do that to a dead person? Really??"*

Then I thought it was a cruel world, and
probably this has happened in the past to test for
physical reaction to pain. We do sternal rubs on
patients who are slow to respond or lethargic, but
not on dead people.

It continued:

*"Listen for absence of heart sounds, feel for carotid pulse, look and listen for absence of spontaneous respirations, record position of the pupils and the absence of papillary light reflex. Record the time at which your exam was completed."*

I closed the book and looked at my watch. It read 0230 hrs. I sighed and went to the floor and climbed a flight of stairs to the 3rd floor. The nurse had the patient's chart ready for me when I walked up to the nurses station.

*"What took you so long Dr. Peters?"* the nurse asked with a smile on her face.

*"Sorry, catching up on how to pronounce someone,"* I sheepishly continued, *"I forgot how to do it from medical school."*

Every July, new interns straight out of med school are thrust into the world of medicine and residency and the bluebloods are all running around learning the hard way, making mistakes, getting taught by the nurses, and the attending physicians all the time. It was a crazy month especially for the nurses who are double and triple checking all the interns' orders.

The silence in the ward was stilled by the darkness. The lowered lights allowed for shadows to cobweb the walls and floors. I found the room and entered.

A small still elderly figure lay in the hospital bed flanked by 2 daughters. Bent over the sides of the bed, the women held their mother's face. I could barely make out some murmuring. What they said, I know not, but I knew what they were saying. They were saying the same thing I would be telling my mother on her death bed.

I would tell her, *"I wish I could have spent more time with you. I will never forget all you have done for me. Thank you for motivating me to keep going even in the rage of the storms. Keep moving against the storms of my heart, my emotions and my mind. Thank you for being the best mother ever. Guiding me the best way I could ever ask for. What I didn't deserve, you always gave me. I love you mom, always and forever."*

I walked to the bed and introduced myself to the daughters. Slightly nervous I asked them their names and their relation to the patient. Greetings aside, I approached the bed with the still patient. With as much gentle and humble respect, I felt for a pulse from the carotids, and then I listened to the heart. Hearing nothing seemed ironic.

Without my hearing aides, I probably would not have been able to hear anything. However, with the strong electronic stethoscope, I can hear more than the normal person. I listened... nothing. It was amazing that this body had a beating heart for many many years, and now... nothing. I felt like I was the gatekeeper to the netherworld.

After checking her pupils, her heart, lungs, temperature, the daughter came to me.

"Is *she gone?*" she asked with resolute determination on her face. To weather the storm, she held firm.

"Yes," I said softly. "*I'm sorry for your loss.*"

She glanced at her aging gaunt and cachectic face, so fragile, framed by white sheets.

"Is *she in Heaven?*"

I looked at her and felt emptiness in my heart. I remember the day Mom introduced me to Jesus and I invited him into my heart. I remember when all the early childhood days in church, Vacation bible school, being baptized. I remember in medical school all the scientific bombardment that made me question my faith.

I remember dad sending me tapes on scientific support for Christianity, and a young earth. My brother directed me to many websites with scientific evidence. Evidence of the flood, stories from the Bible strengthened me.

My mom quoted scripture to me when I called her in despair. She strengthened me through the years. And my mother was so smart, so precious. She born me and raised me. I would love her to be happy forever in that peaceful serenity of Heaven.

I put my hand on the daughter's shoulder and replied, *"I sincerely hope."*

I felt like a turtle moving slowly, purposefully, and without question towards a goal. The call nights became days, and sleep times became wide awake times. My body felt bipolar in a unipolar world. Sometimes I felt like I was hallucinating when in fact, I was sleeping at the hospital, again and again. Sleep in my own little apartment, in my own bed, was like heaven on earth.

And so, the two turtles of my soul continued to walk and make the trail of Internship. Internship was significantly more difficult than medical school, as it seemed that as a medical student you were protected with the "student" status. The fact that you were learning in medical school and that you were a student shielded us from difficult times.

In the intern year, you were a professional being paid a measly salary to work like a slave. It seemed unfair, but also had the most potential for learning. You didn't care about the pay, as much as you cared about making it through the night without something tragic happening to one of your own patients.

I must admit Medicine is an imperfect science. Even though our bodies run on chemical reactions and neurotransmitters, and the sophistication of the brain, we base a lot of our responses on what people say to us, what they react to when we say it, and what they hear.

The interaction between doctor and patient is a relationship that is unfolding. Every minute, however long or short duration the visit, is intricately woven for the betterment of the patient. As a physician to be, I am determined to dedicate my time and energies to the betterment of my fellow humans.

I remember when my mom told me what I was going to be if I became a doctor. She said, *"you will always be a servant of the public as a doctor."* Therefore, we are social servants, public protectors, and patient dignifiers. I know that a fellow human is in pain, because they describe it well. I know when someone cries, it is a true offering up of a sacrifice — a sacrifice of a very personal issue.

A patient can decide to utilize any one means to treat their symptoms. They picked us, and that says a lot.

# Chapter 22

## Hoping in Medicine

O' GREAT SPIRIT
*help me always*
*to speak the truth quietly,*
*to listen with an open mind*
*when others speak,*
*and to remember the peace*
*that may be found in silence.*

Cherokee Prayer

Science continues to evolve with increasing technology and sophistication. Like a cogwheel in time, more discoveries continue to change medicine in many ways. It seems that using robots for surgery was a sci-fi fantasy, and now is utilized in cardiothoracic and obstetric surgery. Its use continues to expand in other fields.

Pharmaceutical companies are continuously developing new medications for therapies, including battling bugs with new antibiotics. The use of MRI and PET scanners evolve to include more and more clinical indications. When once MRI was used for evaluation of brain tissue for cerebrovascular accidents, now is utilized in breast cancer screening.

The genetic code continues to be studied until one day every genetic disease will be categorized and possibly reversed. The future of medicine is as bright as ever, and I remain hopeful for many things. While physicians continue to battle against death and disease, we have to come to terms with death, and not winning that fight. While we have assisted in prolonging life expectancy, we have yet to overcome the inevitable.

The dying are evidence that we as physicians feel we have failed. Each battle brings us down. We can hope that maybe one day we can overcome this fight. Who knows, maybe technology will enable us to live many more years than we ever thought possible. I will continue to hope for all the people.

My wife came to me with a dream she had, she said, *"I had a dream that paw-paw came to me for the first time and gave me a long hug and told me how much he loved me. He has never done that — he always walks around in my dreams."* Her eyes pierced mine with hopeful sincerity, before slowly welling up with tears.

*"Maybe he was giving you a message from Heaven,"* I replied.

*"You think so?"* my wife asked.

I smiled, took a deep breath and replied, *"I sincerely hope."*

I don't pretend to know it all, as it is impossible to know everything about life and death. I am not good at predicting how much time one has to live either. I am not good at acknowledging that medicine has failed. Trying to remain optimistic more than ever now, I tell my 90 year old patients that I want to see them on the cover of the Fort Worth Telegram like that 92 year old golfer recently. They just smile kindly back at me, knowing they are in the twilight hours of their life.

When my 88 year old liver cancer patient was admitted to the hospital, the son asked me if God can cure her. I respect all religions when it comes to medicine. I respect all cultures as much as I know of. I put my hand on his shoulder and replied, *"I sincerely hope."*

I developed a confidence in medicine that no other experience offered. My desire for feedback, and the validation helped me in many ways. Confidence after working so long in the field enabled me to relate quickly with the patient. It was feedback that I strove for. I worked hard to please.

When you study and toil so hard for hours both in and out of the classroom you have a sense of entitlement. In my mind everyone should be respected. However, I have little respect for those who think some should have more or less respect. I have worked hard but I still act humble.

In Medical school, each month the clinical evaluation reports came in and we would see what our preceptors and residents thought of us. The repetitious of positive feedback strengthened me. The difference between what my superiors were saying and what my patients were saying were few and far between. I knew I was doing right with patients. They knew I listened to them and cared with compassion. I believe I was coming full circle, and wouldn't feel inferior anymore.

My dad spent 20 years running stores for Skaggs Alpha Beta. He was good, very good at running them and making them profitable. He was moved from state to state constantly. He told me many things, and one time I relied on one piece of advice.

*"Son, steadfastly defend your reputation because that is all you have."* He said.

Looking back, that seems a little selfish to live by. Now with 2 growing children and a wonderful wife, I think what I really have is in my home and heart. Nothing can take away what is in your heart. Even as I read books to my son and daughter, I think back on the values I have learned to live by, and thank my mom. Without her undying support and faith, I learned to just accept the inevitable. I cannot control what happens to me, but I can control myself. And that turns out to be just enough.

In our last lectures prior to graduation, a series of past professors came and taught us some secrets to their successes. Most of these secrets were good advice, such as: do not place financial interests above the welfare of our patients. Our primary objective of the medical professional is to render service to humanity; reward or financial gain is a subordinate consideration. We are taught what minimal value is. What I would feel comfortable telling my patients? Minimal value of individual gifts are permissive so long as the gifts are related to physician's work.

We learned about the threats to patient privacy. We have a duty to respect the patients' trust and keep information private. Email, answering machine, letters, and test results to a patient via fax can be a threat to privacy. When do we get law enforcement involved? If a patient is an imminent threat to themselves or another individual, we tell law enforcement.

If a family tests positive to a genetic disease and the patient doesn't want us to tell the family what should we do? The duty is to notify the family. Interesting...

I had a sudden idea for a novel. A very rich family, preferably with senators is the central character group. A daughter tests positive for a severe genetic disease. Of course, she doesn't want family to know. The senator has shady dealings, and his coffers use her as leverage to get what they want. Too much disclosure undermines trust.

Hmmmm... it might work.

# Chapter 23

## Many Rains Came on the Iron Horse

*Residency*

*The morning showers*
*Didn't bring flowers*
*Nor did they make it smell*
*Unlike the living hell*
*Life was short and fast*
*I never thought it would last*
*But many rains came worse*
*On my Iron Horse*
*And suffering was stilled*
*To drive took more will,*
*It was all I had,*
*Thank God it wasn't bad*
*The breeze is my best friend.*

*Justus Peters*
*4/12/12*

The Family Medicine Residency program at John Peter Smith (JPS) Hospital in Fort Worth Texas is everything a resident could ask for — great experience, great patients, and great memories. I always called it "the circus." Any county hospital of a metropolitan city is the same: full of trauma, illnesses, and chaos. The next 3 years put hair on my chest literally, and were "man growing," for me.

Compared to internship, JPS really launched my confidence. The anxiety associated with repeating many procedures began to wan. The confidence began to grow, as I was faced with more and more emergencies and disease.

Even to this day, I smile when I drive by JPS on the highway. The memories linger of the all nighters, the surgery rotations, family medicine clinics, the research, and conferences. I can only summarize all the experiences I had at JPS. I will probably not even do JPS any justice.

Dr. Baumer headed the Family Practice program with amazing honesty and integrity, and her advice continues to ring in my ear. With a few minutes in her office, guidance is offered that lasts a lifetime. From what the medical board thinks — *"they expect us to be perfect."* I don't think the medical board is efficient enough to expect any physician to be perfect. But that is just my opinion.

She was the first person that led me to understand how inflammatory bowel disease can be associated with obesity, and also from possibilities of childhood sexual and psychological abuse. I didn't have enough time with her personally to learn a lot, but the little that I did will be treasured.

Dr. Casey is the Residency Director and he has a calm confidence and a witty humor. Tall, lanky, with a balding head and hawkish nose framed by blue eyes, he ambles around with a group of white coats along the wards. He teaches by questioning and illustrating. His black lecture book is filled with perfect grammar and legibility. I don't know if he could survive if he lost that book. The best way to learn is to see one, do one, and then teach one. That is the JPS learning motto. You had to just jump in and learn it. If you were lucky and had a resident who loved to teach, then it made all the difference in the world.

The patient population most commonly had chronic medical issues, including diabetes, hypertension and hypercholesterolemia. Every now and then an anomaly would present itself, such as a young person with a major issue.

One time, I had a mystery case involving a young woman with high blood pressure. Even the depths of medical school learning didn't help with this mystery. I kept asking myself, *"What is a young woman doing with high blood pressure?"*

She denied any issues, no history of medical problems, no family history of high blood pressure or other problems. I could think a few situations that could increase blood pressure in a person, and knew that the work up for secondary causes would be high. Since Dr. Casey was our director, I wanted to get the diagnosis before rounds in the morning.

The severe issues causing high blood pressure include: tumors of the adrenal gland, cerebrovascular accidents, and disruption or obstruction of kidney artery perfusion. Other causes can be pain, illness, and just plain old stress. In a young person with sudden high blood pressure, I was looking at everything. We checked her blood panels, her chemistry, cell count, metabolic panels. I scanned her brain, kidneys and adrenal glands. I did everything trying figure out why she had high blood pressure what little did I know that some people can have high blood pressure when it's just genetics. I couldn't reason with genetics just yet, as I was busy trying to fix people by fixing numbers. With no clear answers among all the studies we did, we discharged her on blood pressure medicine and she was going to follow up.

When she followed up, I still felt like I had failed her, as if to say, "I don't know why you have this disease." I did sympathize with her and tell her she wasn't alone and that we were going to try to take care of her problem together.

Most memorable cases involve the Intensive Care Unit or the Emergency room. Many a call night or a moonlighting night, we had codes, and respiratory failure, and had to do procedures after procedures.

Once, a lethargic hyponatremic patient with respiratory failure and congestive heart failure needed to be stabilized. When an ICU patient started to decompensate, and needed a central line, Dr Casey asked if we could do it, and I said I would do it.

I ran to get all the equipment together and quickly donned my sterile gloves and gown with facemask and shield. To me it felt like the moment I have been waiting for. I wanted to please my boss so much I was willing to jump at the chance with a risky procedure. The benefits outweighed the risks secondary to this patient's grave disease state. Like the many central lines I have tried in the past, this was no different. I was able to obtain a central line via the subclavian vein. I don't think he noticed my beaming face as I aspirated dark venous blood into the syringe.

It was not always like that. I had troubles with the first few central line attempts when I was doing the surgery rotation. My upper level residents were patient as they explained how to do the procedures including the subclavian vein, femoral vein, and the internal jugular vein catheterization technique.

All of the patients that I worked on putting central lines in have my eternal gratitude. A sick person will take whatever help he can get even with a training doctor. I would say a quick prayer for the patient so I would not puncture a lung or an artery. I have punctured arteries instead of veins, but with compression for 5 minutes those small puncture holes seal well. I have accidentally lacerated an artery before and had to repair the arterial wall.

Complications of procedures are always possible. The intention of helping a patient also carries risks, and my job was to always do good, and no harm. My intentions were never to harm any one patient. I look at my patient as family members. I'm dedicated to their health and soul. I have always wanted my patients to be healthy and full of life and vigor, and I support that.

Some call nights I would miss the phone call if a hearing aid battery died while sleeping. Sometimes I would take one hearing aid out to give my ear a break and sleep with the one ear with the hearing aid up so I could hear if a telephone would ring. If that hearing aid battery died, then I didn't hear anything at all.

I preferred keeping my pager on vibrate, because I didn't like sleeping with my hearing aids on. When I was sleeping in the call rooms at JPS overnight, I had to wear my hearing aids. Still, batteries would die and I wouldn't hear anything sometimes. Even overhead calls would be missed by me.

Some residents will tell me that I was paged overhead, which shouldn't have surprised me. But sometimes I forgot I was deaf. We began to resent the pager, regardless of whether we were on call or not. The pager seemed incessant during Surgery trauma call. I could have a waiting list of things to do on people all through the night, including abscess drainages, central line placements, lumbar punctures, wound debridement, and paper work.

In Tarrant County, JPS is the only Level 1 Trauma Center. Therefore, trauma level 1 calls would be coming in every hour on the hour. I saw so many gunshot wounds, respiratory failures, motor vehicle accidents, and things that made me feel like we were in a war zone.

In John Peter Smith Hospital, the family medicine residents ran the medicine teams. We had a hospitalist group that treated patients as well. Being the largest family medicine residency in the country with over 60 residents, we were able to control a lot in the hospital, but we still needed help. JPS had subspecialties in psychiatry, surgery, orthopedics, and interns in all those specialties also had to work with the family medicine residents.

A local medical school also played a huge part in helping with patient care. The amount of experience was not limited to residents, and the students also had a leg up wherever they went. When I was a 3rd year resident, I was teaching medical students to do many of the procedures we learned as interns. Therefore medical students learning through JPS were way more experienced than the norm.

The greatest gift my residency training gave me was to appreciate life. Life is fragile, and everyday is a gift. The experiences and emotional trauma from ER are breath-taking. Life as a deaf physician had less importance to me than life it-self. But I'll remember that when call was over, and we laid the pager in someone else's hands, we felt lifted to enjoy that life. And walking out-side into the sun light was like being born again.

# Chapter 24

## Awakening

*Poem*

*A shining city in sunset*
*Yet coldness in the rain,*
*The church keeps warm from the wet,*
*And comfort from the pain.*
*Wiry fast and guile,*
*The desert now with grass,*
*With modernistic styles,*
*And a poetic class.*
*A pretty rock and drive*
*And by the Sea of Dead,*
*Up the hill we then arrive,*
*We turn and turn no straight ahead.*
*A turn and then a wall,*
*We cared among the poor,*
*A baby girl with her doll,*
*The sewage on the floor.*
*The gardens bloom down low,*
*In fertile valleys few,*
*And mountains many we go,*
*In fog of morning dew.*
*The path a prophet walked,*
*The hill where he died,*
*In remembrance many flocked,*
*The many spirits fly.*

*Justus Peters MD*

Dr. David McRay invited me on a trip to Israel and Palestine for a month. Always wanting to travel, I didn't hesitate to volunteer. The trip opened my eyes onto the differences in medicine in modern technologically advanced Israel, and the Occupied Territories of the West Bank.

We spent our first night near the Old City in Jerusalem, and an adventure began. We arrived with the rains, and had dinner at the Christmas Hotel just outside the old city. Dr. McRay points out where he lived as a child while his father worked as an archeologist. We ate kibble, sudjuk, pita, hummus, and falafel. Oh what a great first true Middle Eastern meal.

As a history buff, I had to learn everything I could about Israel and Palestine. I learned about how the city had changed since its prime during Solomon's reign, to the Jewish Revolt and the Roman occupation. I learned of the wars between the Crusaders and the Muslims, and finally the Six Day War which ended with the International Green Line, and later the Yom Kippur war which enabled Israel to expand its borders more.

Being without warm showers was eye opening, as I had never lived without warm water before. I soon appreciated so much from home. The regularity and normalcy of everyday life dissolved like a morning fog with each passing day in Israel.

The first week we spent in Israel in Beer Sheva, the 7th largest city of the Negev Desert. Soroka Medical Center, where we worked and toured, was the 4th largest in Israel. Dr. Aya Biderman, Family Medicine Staff at Yud Alef Clinic, hosted us all week. She gave me Hebrew lessons every day. Like learning a new culture, it was exciting to be in a new world. I was studying medicine and culture, as well as language. My favorite words were; *"Shalom," "Mashlomcha,"* (how are you male), *"Mashlomech,"* (how are you female), *"Beseder,"* (ok), and *"Metzuyan!"* (excellent!). Dr. Biderman made Mousaka at her home and was a wonderful hostess.

Beer Sheva was where the British defeated the Turks in World War 1. It was also the site of Israel defense in its War of Independence in 1948. Ben Gurion University was a very modern and beautiful campus, and it was gated and watched over by armed guards. It was a new experience to have young men and women with large automatic weapons looking at your passport.

We visited the Museum of Bedouin Culture and Bedouin village of Lakiya where we could see how they did their world class weaving. This modern city in the desert was starkly contrasted with what I was about to see a few miles away across a long tall wall.

The medical system in Israel was very impressive, ranked 28th in the world by the World Health Organization. It is both universal and compulsory and is administered by a small number of Health Management Organizations funded from the government.

In contrast, Palestine per capita spending for healthcare is $138, vs. $5000 in the US. A lot of medical care relies on foreign aid and non-governmental organizations (NGOs). The weak systems for licensing and continuing education allow for some under-qualified health care providers. The coordination and implementation of policies and programs is poor system wide.

Endemic to Palestine was the persistence of gastroenteric and parasitic diseases, hepatitis A, respiratory infections and meningitis. Access to healthcare has declined causing increase in malnutrition and rising rates of chronic diseases.

After the first week, we travelled down through the beautiful mountains in the Negev further through to a small clinic in Yokvata north of Eilat. A large crater 300 meters deep and 40km long was experienced during the drive.

Crossing the border into Jordan and then travelling by taxi to Petra, we stopped and stayed at the Valentine Hotel. Large ornamental rugs adorned the walls. A small room to the side had Indiana Jones movie that showed the scene of the Treasury where he went to find the Holy Grail.

Bruce Feiler wrote in his wonderful book, "Walking the Bible," that Petra, the name itself evokes magic, like "Shangri La, Xanadu or Timbuktu. It is known as the "Boutinneire" of the Middle East, a shimmering illusory place, carved out of salmon colored mountains. This is where the Nabateans thrived for 400 years during the time of Christ.

The next day we toured Petra, starting down at the mouth of the wadi, walking for about a half mile before coming to the awesome Treasury which was in the famous scene on Indiana Jones movie. I was amazed and overwhelmed. The insides of these large porticos were plain, yet the salmon colored stones had various tints and shades that made the walls appear alive and full of history.

We hiked up the High Sacrificial Place and came down to the Roman Theatre, where we could see the Urn Tomb.

One trip that couldn't be missed was the Monastery. The donkey renters said there were 950 steps. They added that it would take me an hour without a donkey to make it to the top, and 20 minutes with a donkey. Never wanting to drop a challenge, I walked up alone, and made it in 20 minutes without a donkey.

We spent the next 3 weeks in Palestine, or what is technically called the Occupied Territories. In Ramallah, the pride of Palestine, we stayed with a medical care NGO, the Palestine Medical Relief Society. We travelled the villages learning of the medical systems and disease management. One of the staff members at the Sheik Zayed hospital became a dear friend, Dr. Nasser. He taught me Arabic, and I spoke as much as I could, learning and writing and speaking it with the local patients.

I even learned a little of the politics that occurred in Palestine regarding Fatah and Hamas. Most of the physicians I met were Christians. The citizens, whether they were Christian or Muslim were charming, sociable, and friendly.

Sheikh Zayed Hospital, which is the only emergency hospital in the West Bank and Gaza, has five resident doctors, 30 outside doctors providing special medical services, and 27 nurses who serve over 270,000 Palestinians. When we travelled around Israel to Bethlehem, the distance in a straight line could have gotten us there in 30 minutes, but travelling around the wall and through back roads got us there at about 2 hours.

This month long adventure opened my eyes on many subjects, namely the water crisis in Palestine and its effect on health. The World Health Organization reports that for good health, a single citizen should have a consumption of about 100 liters a day. The Palestinians were living on only 55.

In America, we don't see a lot of hepatitis because our water filtering systems are top of the line. In Palestine, even boiling water doesn't stop the endemic diseases such as cholera, hepatitis, and amoebic dystentery. One village we visited, Beit Furik had no health clinic and access to only two local doctors which are actually shared with another village.

When I returned from Israel, Donnette remembers how "efficient" I was at doing so many things around the house. I was laundering and ironing my clothes. She actually wants to send me again so that I can return a "changed man," again. I had a more worldly view that couldn't be persuaded by the media on television.

Whatever politics that were shaping the future of Israel and Palestine were not a concern, until after this trip. Now having learned about both countries, I have a deep respect for both Israel and Palestine, and hope that they can come to some peace agreement.

If history repeats itself, peace in Israel can be obtained. It is all relative however, depending on your definition of peace. In the western frontier here in America, the settlers fought with the Native Americans until peace was obtained. Trapped in the wars and the changing cultures are a people who try to get by with what they have. Like the Native Americans, the Palestinians lived their lives with rich heritage and tradition.

Now America takes pride in its Native American heritage. One day Israel will take pride in its Palestinian heritage. The Jewish heritage is so rich and immense, yet it won't take away from sharing and respecting what there once was in their land. Just as the Native Americans developed a bond with the United States, and a strong sense of pride, the Palestinians can develop the same with the Israelis. It will just take time.

# Chapter 25

## A Dragon-Fly

*Do you remember me?*
*Drawing all your friends?*
*The many colored seas,*
*And watching til the end,*
*Sunsets by and by,*
*A joy you have made.*
*My Dragon Fly,*
*Never will I fade.*

Justus Peters
4/13/2012

Now practicing at Pecan Family Medical Center, I have both many success and failure stories. Failure in my mind is the loss of a patient to death. Although this is normal, as a physician, it is my duty to fight it until I can't anymore. So it is ok that I am hard on myself for my patients. It is my personal burden to bear.

Most of my patient encounters are small but happy success stories. I enjoy more success stories by far. If a chronic disease is what I am fighting, so be it. I might not succeed in some of those battles, but I enjoy taking care of the people whatever their problem is.

Helping my old golfer patients with their little aches and pains enables them to share their latest score with me. Normalizing a blood pressure which decreases the chance for heart attack or stroke enables a patient to enjoy life with less risk. Assisting with weight loss enables patients to live healthy lifestyles. Teaching patients the benefits of preventive maintenance, skin care, and exercise all point to importance of the medical home.

Every now and then I get to give a little Botox to fight signs of aging. My patients love that stuff.

I probably never thought I would be doing Medicine forever, but so far it is very enriching and challenging. I respect the human body not only for its tenacity, but also for its many mysteries. The human body can take so much affliction before succumbing to death. I've seen horrible accidents almost claim lives, and watch them heal in rehab after months of physical therapy. Life is like ebb and flow, with those who die might come back if we are lucky enough to have them in the ER.

One of my happiest moments after graduation from residency was in the saving of my first major cardiac arrest patient

I remember that first major code in the ER clearly. A young gentleman about 55 years old came in with chest pain. He seemed too young for a major heart attack, but we worked him up anyway. So while we are working him, getting blood draws, EKGs, and X-rays, all of a sudden he stiffens in the stretcher, and his eyes roll backward. His cardiac monitor showed ventricular fibrillation.

Ventricular fibrillation, or V-fib for short, is where the parts of the heart that pumps blood all over the body, and to the lungs just quivers instead of pump. This is called fibrillation. The same thing can happen to the atrium, but that is not fatal. V-fib is 100% fatal unless shocked out of rhythm to a normal sinus rhythm.

We immediately shocked him at 200 J and the monitor showed normal sinus rhythm, and he came back. He nearly died, and he was back, just like that. I explained to him what we just did, and told him, that he had to go to a cardiologist to get a heart cath right away.

When he started vomiting, we had to intubate him so we could protect his airway, and he was immediately life-flighted up to the metroplex. This success story was very fulfilling. I had another experience but instead of ventricular fibrillation, the man had atrial fibrillation.

He was 85 years old, and he had unstable atrial fibrillation with rapid ventricular rate. This means his blood pressure is too low to sustain his life. His blood pressure was 60 systolic over 40 and he had altered mental status. So we immediately shocked him at 50 J and he came back to a regular rate controlled atrial fibrillation. His mental status came back right away although he was very upset and angry about the pain from the shock. But he was alive.

I now have the opportunity to evaluate children for Shriner's Hospitals. Although I am not an ortho surgeon, I still work with orthopedics nearly on a daily basis. Children with scoliosis and club foot are common referrals to these specialty hospitals. As a Shriner, I know I am doing my part in helping children walk again.

I become very close to my patients here at Pecan Family Medical Center and I treat them like my own children and family. And I've lost some dear friends through whether from lung cancer or severe liver failure. But it was an honor to treat them and be there for them in their final moments of life.

My patients are always full of great advice in life, and I learn so much from them. My favorite quote is, „if it's not one thing, it's your mother." I have the best family, and in each person that I treat, I realize that they are giving me a part of themselves, and that trust is empowering, more than any other possible gift.

I feel like I have grown more mature in this current leg of my journey of medicine. Although there will be many hills and mountains to overcome still I look forward to the challenges that medicine will bring me

Hopefully I will continue serving the people and preserving their integrity, dignity, as well as their health. I hope that I will continue to serve, continuing the promise to the Oath, and that I will not detour.

# About the Author

Dr. Justus Peters MD is a Family Physician in Glen Rose Texas. He currently treats "Pediatrics to Geriatrics," in Pecan Plantation in Granbury. He lives with his wife and many children, 2 human, 2 dogs, 3 cats, and a fish. He can be emailed at runsinthewynd@gmail.com, or follow him on Twitter @askjustusmd. He writes a blog www.askjustusmd.blogspot.com

# Acknowledgements

All of this would not have been possible without the support and love from my family, especially my wife, Donnette, in her seemingly infinite patience, caring, and understanding. Thanks to my children Anna and Luke who help me laugh at the world sometimes. Thank you all so much, and I of course love you.

A special thanks to Alexander Becker, super talented editor who put the whole package together-the formatting, cover, book, and everything else he touches. Super thanks.

Thanks to Createspace.com and publishing consultant Travis Craine for all the input and publishing efforts. The book would just be another stack on my desk uncompleted without you all.

I am remiss if I didn't mention my parents Don and Sandra Peters, who guided me through the hard years-thank you and I love you both dearly.

Every author has a literary hero, and I'd like to thank Dean Koontz whose novels were the first I ever read, and in doing so developed a sense of writing ability. Thanks for your input and guidance.

CPSIA information can be obtained at www.ICGtesting.com
Printed in the USA
LVOW121537261012

304624LV00001B/47/P